About the Author

Brett Hennig is a director and co-founder of the Sortition Foundation, whose aim is to promote the ideas within *The End of Politicians: Time for a Real Democracy* and institute the use of stratified, random selection (also called sortition) in government.

Before co-founding the Sortition Foundation, he wore a variety of hats: as a taxi driver, a software engineer, a social justice activist, a mathematics tutor and the primary carer of four boys – the first of whom arrived a year after he obtained his PhD in astrophysics.

After spending several disheartening years trying to influence political decisions, from both inside and outside the system, he became inspired by Michael Hardt and Antonio Negri's trilogy on political philosophy and began investigating and researching network forms of democracy. This book is the result of those years of work.

THE END OF POLITICIANS

THE END OF POLITICIANS

TIME FOR A REAL DEMOCRACY

BRETT HENNIG

Unbound

This edition first published in 2017

Unbound

6th Floor Mutual House, 70 Conduit Street, London W1S 2GF

www.unbound.com

ISBN (eBook): 978-1-911586-17-3

ISBN (Paperback): 978-1-911586-10-4

Design by Mecob

Cover image:

© Shutterstock.com / edel

This book was produced using Pressbooks.com, and PDF rendering was
done by PrinceXML.

Printed and bound in Great Britian by Clays Ltd, Elcograf S.p.A.

Dear Reader,

The book you are holding came about in a rather different way to most others. It was funded directly by readers through a new website: Unbound.

Unbound is the creation of three writers. We started the company because we believed there had to be a better deal for both writers and readers. On the Unbound website, authors share the ideas for the books they want to write directly with readers. If enough of you support the book by pledging for it in advance, we produce a beautifully bound special subscribers' edition and distribute a regular edition and e-book wherever books are sold, in shops and online.

This new way of publishing is actually a very old idea (Samuel Johnson funded his dictionary this way). We're just using the Internet to build each writer a network of patrons. Here, at the back of this book, you'll find the names of all the people who made it happen.

Publishing in this way means readers are no longer just passive consumers of the books they buy, and authors are free to write the books they really want. They get a much fairer return too: half the profits their books generate, rather than a tiny percentage of the cover price.

If you're not yet a subscriber, we hope that you'll want to join our publishing revolution and have your name listed in one of our books in the future. To get you started, here is a £5 discount on your first pledge. Just visit unbound.com, make your pledge and type EOPOL17 in the promo code box when you check out.

Thank you for your support,

Dan, Justin and John
Founders, Unbound

Super Patrons

Tom Lord
Carlo Lugaro
Paolo Lugaro
Silvio Lugaro
Sarah Maddison
Spiro Metaxas
John Mitchinson
Tim Parrington
David Patten
Anne Pattillo
Joanne Petrovic
Paolo Piagi
Roberto Piscetta
Justin Pollard
Onno Pols
Christopher Rayner
Alan Rhys Evans
Rod Rippin
Roger Sharp
Abram Sharyar
Antonio Siciliano
Ania Sieracka
Peter Stone
Yumi Stynes
Nivek Thompson
Emiel van der Herberg
David Week
Tina Wilkins
Kylie Wilkinson
Trent Williams
Amy Williams
Bettina Wittneben
Arpad Zsoldos

'We have frequently printed the word Democracy. Yet I cannot too often repeat that it is a word the real gist of which still sleeps, quite unawaken'd, notwithstanding the resonance and the many angry tempests out of which its syllables have come, from pen or tongue. It is a great word, whose history, I suppose, remains unwritten, because that history has yet to be enacted.'

Walt Whitman, *Democratic Vistas*

Contents

Part IV: Time to Change

List of Figures

Praise for The End of Politicians

Darn! This is the book I wish I had written. Compelling, inspiring, evidence-based. Hennig explains how democracy got us into this mess, and how we can fix it.
—Professor Lyn Carson, University of Sydney, Director of the
newDemocracy Foundation

Do you believe holding elections every couple of years means you live in a democracy? Short, powerfully argued and carefully researched, Hennig shows how elections have for a long time been known to serve the interests of the powerful – and how ordinary citizens can regain control of their government.
—Professor Manuel Arriaga, New York University, author of
Rebooting Democracy: A Citizen's Guide to Reinventing Politics

Hennig takes stock of democracy in the past and present. His bold assessment will enable us to step out of the shadows of the political elite. Hennig does not stop there, however. In a fast-forward to the future, he outlines ways and systems that will make the dream of democracy come true. This book is an energy drink for social action.
—Dr Bettina Wittneben, University of Oxford

The End of Politicians *provides a powerful critique of the democratic deficits inherent in all forms of electoral democracy. But it does much more than explore the undemocratic qualities of electoral democracy; it proposes a compelling and provocative alternative – the random selection of ordinary citizens to serve as fully empowered legislators. Whether one agrees with this or not, the clarity of the argument will generate productive debate.*
—Professor Erik Olin Wright, University of Wisconsin-Madison, author of *Envisioning Real Utopias*

Hennig has the right idea: democracy requires innovation at any age, but especially this one. The End of Politicians *doesn't call for an end to politics, but rather to antiquated institutions over-reliant on a small number of elected leaders. That system brought us this far, but Hennig reviews many of the alternatives that are already reshaping governance, by injecting the wider public back into public life – not as a mobilized mob, but through more deliberative bodies. Reading this book gives a glimpse of what's already*

changing and what lies on – or just beyond – the horizon of democratic political reform.
    —Professor John Gastil, Penn State University, author of *Democracy in Small Groups*

Introduction: Democracy Mutates

On 30 January 1649, King Charles I of England mounted a platform at Whitehall in London, in front of thousands of spectators, and placed his head on a chopping block before a masked executioner. Not only was he about to die, but the idea that kings had a God-given right to rule was also about to take a lethal blow. After the axe descended and blood spurted across the platform, his decapitated head was held high for all to see. The belief that specific people were predestined to rule would never again go unquestioned.

The execution occurred half a century after Charles's father, James VI of Scotland, later to be crowned King James I of England, had explicitly invoked the divine right of kings to justify the absolute power of monarchs. In *The True Law of Free Monarchies*, James I deduced, from a creative interpretation of the Bible, that kings were higher beings than other men. Many rulers, before and since, have sought to legitimise their position of power through a variety of claims; the theory of divine right was just one such attempt.

Almost a century and a half after Charles's execution, the secondary idea that lineage, at least for the firstborn son, bestowed legitimacy on a ruler also died – this time under the executioner's guillotine instead of his axe. In Paris, on 21 January 1793, Louis XVI mounted a scaffold in Place de la Révolution and was beheaded. The subsequent Reign of Terror would see tens of thousands of the French nobility and aristocracy and other political opponents executed as 'enemies' of the revolution.

Execution was one sure and definitive way of abolishing inherited aristocratic privilege, one of the principal demands and consequences of the French Revolution. For many years, the nobility had mismanaged the French state and its finances, and the rise of a budding capitalist class – in many cases richer than the aristocrats, yet still excluded from governmental positions of power – explicitly contradicted the feudal belief that inequality was somehow 'natural' or 'God-willed'. It became increasingly obvious that ability did not necessarily flow through the bloodlines of aristocratic families. After the French Revolution, heredity would no longer be seen as an adequate justification for rule. Power was not divine, and it was not even a birthright.[1]

History, however, does not proceed in straight lines. The ebb and flow of ideas does not stop, and ideas are easily trampled by those wishing to consolidate positions of power. The Enlightenment hope that humanity is continually approaching a state of perfection was destroyed during the first, barbaric half of the 20th century; progress is never assured in perpetuity.

In England, Oliver Cromwell (1599–1658), one of the principal commanders in the New Model Army during the English Civil War, a vehement anti-royalist and one of the signatories of Charles I's death warrant, later accepted the title of Lord Protector of the Commonwealth of England, Scotland and Ireland 'by the Grace of God'. This was a lifetime position, giving him the right to choose his son as successor. His authoritarian rule soon ended, and less than two years after his death the monarchy, in the person of Charles II, was restored. The French, after the astounding rise of a soldier, Napoleon Bonaparte, to the position of First Consul and then Emperor of France, and the resulting destruction of large swathes of Europe, also returned to monarchy in 1814.

Yet in retrospect, it can be seen that the tide had turned. Attempts to justify the concentration of power into very few hands were increasingly being challenged. The idea of rule with the consent of all citizens, who were to be considered political equals, was slowly spreading.

This would mark a fundamental shift in the popular conception of legitimate rule. The persistent claim by unaccountable leaders that they, for various reasons, deserved to be the ones making and changing the laws would soon be commonly met with cynicism. The justifications given by monarchs and the aristocratic ruling classes appeared little more than blatant attempts to maintain positions of privilege and wealth.

More revolutions followed. Eric Hobsbawm highlights three major 'waves of revolution' that swept across Europe between 1815 and 1848 alone.[2] The dramatic political and economic changes of the late 18th and 19th centuries continued unabated. After much brutal and inevitably violent struggle, popular republican governments gradually spread and took control of the institutions and levers of power in many nation states. Democracy was painfully reborn as people rediscovered a taste for a term buried in antiquity.

Not that any of the governments of the time would be called democratic by modern standards, where democracy requires, at a bare minimum, suffrage for the vast majority of adults permanently residing within a nation state. In France, in 1789–90, the male property-owning authors of the first French constitution (adopted in 1791) introduced the concept of *active* citizenship – adults who paid a specified minimum of taxes – to exclude women and the impoverished rabble from voting and standing for election. Those 'deprived of political rights for legitimate reasons', such as women, children and the poor, were believed unable to make informed decisions since they had no active (i.e., monetary) stake in the nation's well-being.[3] The franchise at the time was approximately one-sixth of the adult population, profoundly at odds with the first article of the *Declaration of the Rights of Man and of the Citizen*, which states: 'Men are born and remain free and equal in rights.' However, the election for the French National Convention in 1792 included provisions for all males over the age of 25 to vote, and is therefore considered the first example of universal male suffrage. It was a very short-lived experiment with a low voter turnout. 'The constitution-makers of 1795 did not resurrect the category of active citizens elaborated in 1790, but they put effective voting power, that of the second assemblies, squarely in the hands of substantial property owners... Not until 1848 was this principle challenged', says William Doyle.[4] All male taxpayers over the age of 21 could vote for the 'electors', who were then responsible for electing the legislators. The electors, however, had to own property equivalent to 100 to 200 days of unskilled labour, making them an even more exclusive club than those of the 1791 constitution.

In the United States of America there were, for many years, similar restrictions. The irony of the mid-18th-century revolutionary slogan 'No taxation without representation' was that in the new republic there would be little to no representation for the majority of people who were poor and therefore did not pay taxes.[5] Some 80 years after the American Revolutionary War, during Abraham Lincoln's presidency of 1861–65, 'government of the people, by the people, for the people' still excluded women, African-Americans and Native Americans from voting, and the imposition of poll taxes and literacy tests designed to disenfranchise African-Americans and the poor were still being challenged in US courts as late as 1966.[6] The historic piece of legislation that ended these practices, the Voting Rights Act of 1965, has since been 'gutted' by a US Supreme Court decision of 2013, immediately leading to the reimposition of various obstacles to voting.[7]

Yet, despite their severe shortcomings when measured against our modern democratic ideals, the late-18th- and 19th-century experiments in parliamentary government marked the consolidation of the idea that legitimate government required the assent of more than just the one (monarchy) or the few (aristocracy); it required the participation of the many, even though exactly how many was fiercely contested and disputed.

That this revolution in attitudes towards what defines legitimate rule ran on parallel tracks with the scientific and industrial revolutions and the rise and domination of capitalism is hardly surprising. The massive expansion and rollout of the railway, the telegraph and Enlightenment ideals were accompanied by the overthrow of the *ancien régime* of privilege based on feudalism, serfdom and the strict hierarchical social relations of peasant and gentry. A new class of wealthy entrepreneurs clearly disproved the notion that competence was an inherited trait. It also gave them their new qualification for rule: wealth. Money replaced lineage as a prerequisite for participation in government, and as women were in general disallowed from owning anything, their exclusion was automatic. These were indeed 'republics of property'.[8]

What can be said for certain is that democracy was neither intended, nor even vaguely anticipated, in the early days of legislative parliaments. In the US, the majority of the Founding Fathers were profoundly anti-democratic. At the Philadelphia Constitutional Convention in 1787, a proposal requesting a clause detailing property (wealth) qualifications for legislators was supported by 90 per cent of the attendees. It was only dropped for reasons of expediency: they could not agree on the precise details, and most US states already implemented property qualifications, so there was no need to replicate them at the national level.[9] Another feature designed to stem the influence of citizens was indirect election, whereby national senators, the president and vice-president were elected exclusively by state representatives. Not until the 17th Amendment of the Constitution, in 1913, was this replaced by direct election of senators; the president and vice-president continue to be indirectly elected through the electoral college system.[10]

In the UK, the original parliamentary system that existed to constrain the powers of monarchs included tax qualifications on the right to vote, with even higher qualifications to stand as a candidate, and the only taxes were usually on property.[11] Initially, the minimal expansions of the franchise were often attempts to co-opt more of the rich and powerful into the governing elite. Sometimes it was a compromise between monarchs needing funds for war and the wealthy wanting greater power, at other times a Machiavellian way to split a threatening opposition by incorporating a subset of them.

Even as increasing popular agitation meant the general expansion of the franchise to all male adults in the mid to late 19th century seemed inevitable, it is interesting to note that these calls were often heeded by conservative politicians, for reasons such as differentiating themselves from opponents within their own party. Eventually, mass protests and civil disobedience by the suffragettes and the American civil rights movement put the political inclusion of women and African-Americans squarely on the agenda.

Slowly, often violently, a haphazard 'fusion of forces... dragged Europe towards much more democratic forms of representative government', where most of the (adult) people exercised at least some form of minimal control over their rulers through regular, open, fair and competitive elections.[12] Today, in approximately half of the world's modern nation states, representative democracy and universal suffrage have triumphed as the basis of legitimate government. Politicians in democratic states can at least claim that it is the people deciding who is to make and modify the laws, and confidently reject the original 'legitimate' exclusions based on gender, wealth or skin colour. The improbable became the possible, and now democracy is the common demand of all who wish to escape the yoke of dictatorship or authoritarian regime.

This strange and illuminating story of the surprising, unintended and recent ideological success of the reincarnated concept of democracy in the last few hundred years, and its impressive contemporary history, is revisited in more detail in Chapters One to Three of Part One, 'Representative Democracy'.

Francis Fukuyama asserted, in 1989, that we are 'witnessing... the end point of mankind's ideological evolution and the universalization of Western liberal democracy as the final form of human government'.[13] A tour of the history of democracy will cast doubt on this assertion. No society is static. If anything, taking the long view will make change seem inevitable. Electoral democracy is not a terminus. The struggle for more legitimate forms of government will continue. The history of democracy shows that this very recent governmental form, which is less than a century old if we date it from the time of widespread universal adult suffrage, will surely mutate and evolve again. The question is this: how will it mutate and what will it evolve into?

Many obvious challenges to democracy exist, both from within and outside of democratic states. Authoritarian regimes such as China, Saudi Arabia and North Korea continue to claim legitimacy from paternalistic notions of guardianship, arguing that the superior knowledge and ideological or religious purity of their leaders allow them to better govern in the interests and for the betterment of the people. China claims, for instance, in Articles 1, 2 and 14 of The Constitution of the People's Republic of China, to be a 'state under the people's democratic dictatorship' where 'All power in the People's Republic of China belongs to the people' and 'The state... gradually improves the material and cultural life of the people.' In the semi-theocratic regime of the Islamic Republic of Iran a 'Guardian Council' and an 'Assembly of Experts of Islamic Scholars' secure equity and justice for the people as its leadership is qualified in regard to the Qur'an, according to their 1979 constitution. North Korea's official title, the 'Democratic People's Republic of Korea', is perhaps the best example of democratic hubris, although the words in the preamble to its constitution cannot be very far behind: that Kim Il Sung 'regards the idea of "Serving the people as heaven" as his motto'.[14]

A number of leaders, particularly in the developing world, look admiringly at the model of Chinese autocracy.[15] Robert Dahl, the doyen of democracy studies in the United States, says guardianship 'has always been the major rival to democratic ideas... [The guardians] simply deny that ordinary people are competent to govern themselves'.[16] It is noteworthy that even authoritarian regimes strenuously promote the idea of their own legitimacy, through a varying combination of bribery, propaganda, censorship and oppression. It matters what the people think: they must be made to understand that the rulers are ruling in the people's best interests.[17]

Other challenges to democracy lie in the all-too-apparent failures of, general disaffection with and cynicism towards the modern representative system and its politicians. In survey after survey people invariably rank 'politician' as one of the least trustworthy and most dishonest of professions, along with 'car salesman' and 'real estate agent'.[18] Voter exit polls in 2014 in the US found that 'about 8 in 10 Americans disapprove of how Congress is handling its job'.[19] Anthony King, in *Who Governs Britain?*, notes that: 'For anyone searching for scapegoats, politicians as a class make easy prey. They always have. Unfortunately, a large proportion of them bring it on themselves.'[20]

These high levels of political disaffection have been accompanied by plummeting membership of political parties in most democratic states. Precise numbers are impossible to come by due to party secrecy, but it has been estimated that in the UK in the 1950s Labour membership was more than a million, while the Conservatives had perhaps 2.8 million members.[21] Even with the recent (probably temporary) surge that doubled Labour Party membership when Jeremy Corbyn was elected leader in 2015, the long-term trend can still be characterised as a 'collapse' – even more so since, during the same period, the overall population of the UK increased by more than 20 per cent. Democratic Audit, in their 2012 report, *How Democratic is the UK?*, put it like this:

> Long-term survey evidence suggests that the public trust politicians and political parties less and less... and have growing concerns about levels of corruption in politics and government... [T]here are very firm grounds to suggest that the power which large corporations and wealthy individuals now wield on the UK political system is unprecedented... All measures of popular engagement with, and attitudes towards, representative democracy show a clear decline since the 1970s. Whether the measures we adopt are turnout in elections, membership of political parties, voter identification with political parties, or public faith in the system of government, the pattern is the same...[22]

Paradoxically, this retreat of ordinary people from formal politics has made it even harder for politicians to make the difficult decisions required to address the multiple economic, climatic and social crises afflicting our times. Reduced public participation increases the sphere of influence of special-interest groups, corporations and their paid lobbyists, the mainstream media and highly ideological party activists. When party membership dues decline, the importance of large donations from wealthy donors and corporations increases. This capture of the political process, further detailed in Chapters Four and Five, derails any genuine attempt to tackle the problems, especially if they conflict with corporate or donor interests.

This leaves the machinations of state to a small class of politicians, journalists and lobbyists, who, at least until the rise of social media in the last decade, pandered to traditional media conglomerates as the best way to access and influence potential voters. When the US president needs to tweet 'The gun lobby may be holding Congress hostage, but they can't hold America hostage', it would seem that our democracy has been captured by special interests.[23]

Are these problems merely symptoms of the inevitable gap

between our democratic ideals and its messy reality? Apathy and cynicism are easy to understand in the face of recurrent scandals, such as the breathtaking corruption and favours, payments and kickbacks among the media, the police and politicians exposed by the police inquiries related to the News International phone-hacking scandal and resulting Leveson Inquiry in the UK in 2011–12 (more details of this and the scandals below are given in Chapter Four). Other examples include the police investigation associated with the cash-for-peerages scandal in the UK's House of Lords in 2006 and the dubious appointments and thwarting of justice by recent US presidents. Allegations of cronyism were levelled at President G. W. Bush after he appointed a friend, Michael D. Brown, to direct the Federal Emergency Management Agency and it so spectacularly failed to respond adequately to Hurricane Katrina in 2005. Bush also commuted the prison sentence of a loyal subordinate (Lewis 'Scooter' Libby), who pleaded guilty to a vengeful leak after an ambassador questioned the factual basis of the Iraq War – the so-called Plame Affair. President Obama continued the practice of awarding plush ambassadorial appointments to his most effective fundraisers, such as Hollywood producer Colleen Bell, who knew next to nothing about Hungary, the country she was heading to.[24] With the constant flow of scandal, the integrity of politicians and the political process is easy to doubt.

Is the only hope to react *ex post facto* to these most egregious perversions of democracy? Or do they form part of a broader pattern indicating the need to find new forms of legitimacy and new ways to govern ourselves?

Whatever the answer to these questions, it is important to remember that democracy *has* triumphed as an ideal: it is now the indisputable norm in western society. It has become a 'global political language' and 'a global value'.[25] However, as Russell Dalton states:

> Even though contemporary publics express decreasing confidence in democratic politicians, parties and parliaments... [m]ost people remain committed to the democratic ideal; if anything, these sentiments have apparently strengthened as satisfaction with the actuality of democratic politics has decreased.[26]

People support democracy, but they are unsatisfied with its current incarnation.[27] Indeed, after years of spectacular technological advance, the current form of democracy looks like a dinosaur. In John Keane's words: 'Politicians, parties and parliaments began to look and feel like fossils – not quite trilobites, but certainly residues from better times.'[28] Claims that representative democracy as it now stands is the best we can possibly hope for ring hollow.

Just as modern representative democracy and the industrial revolution emerged simultaneously, another revolutionary change in the meaning and practice of legitimate government is anticipated as the information and communications revolution pushes society along on a wave of digital innovation.

If Part One of this book lays the historical foundation, Part Two sets the contemporary context. Change will happen; the question is, how? The emergence of today's highly networked economic, cultural and social structures and processes are having a profound effect on politics. As new forms and technologies of inclusion open up, and rapidly become commonplace, democracy is being revolutionised.

Not all of these changes are positive, but we can attempt to understand and anticipate the risks. And by combining the positive aspects of our network society with other recent trends in democratic theory and practice, such as the techniques and analysis of deliberative democracy – detailed in Chapter Eleven – these changes hold out much hope that many of the deficits of our current form of democracy can be overcome.

How people should live together is the key question that democracy tries to answer. We have arrived at the historical juncture where at least half of the people on the planet agree that the formulation of a *legitimate* answer to that question should (in theory) involve every adult on an equal basis – even though 'involve' and 'equal' are deceptively slippery terms. In some minimal sense (about which much more will be said in Parts One and Three) it currently means that each person's vote should count equally so that we collectively decide which representatives should determine, on our behalf, the laws that govern how we live together. However, even though the legal struggle for universal suffrage has been won, it often feels like the political battle for popular control of our parliaments has been lost. People vote, but a wealthy few hold the purse strings of the parties whose leaders take power: just 76 people accounted for nearly half of all individual and corporate donations to political parties in the run-up to the 2015 UK election, and 'around 130 families and their businesses accounted for more than half the money raised by Republican candidates' in the early days of the 2016 US primaries.[29] Elections always have been, and presumably always will be, expensive affairs. The history of democracy shows how money has both dominated and polluted politics ever since democracy's modern revival. Whether inherited, earned or 'donated' to a political party, money buys access and influence.

Could a real democracy of the people increase the legitimacy of parliaments while avoiding the pitfalls of the current version of representative democracy? The answer to this question, elaborated in Parts Three and Four, is an emphatic yes. With an appreciation of how and why the franchise was extended, combined with a better understanding of the opportunities and risks inherent in the new participatory social forms and deliberative processes, it is possible to formulate a positive answer to the question of whether the legitimacy of the laws that govern and bind us can be further increased.

Part Three outlines how to fix our broken politics. It explains how a real democracy would eliminate politicians and replace them with a representative network of randomly selected, ordinary citizens. The surprising yet overwhelming evidence from the many recent citizens' assemblies, detailed in Chapters Eleven and Twelve, is that they work: with unbiased, transparent and collaborative processes ordinary people can and do make substantive, informed and balanced decisions over an extensive range of complex policy areas. Random selection of people to political posts – known as 'sortition' – is as old as democracy itself. Both its historical usage and its impressive contemporary revival are detailed in Chapters Twelve and Thirteen, and it is shown that sortition has been and still is an accountable, legitimate and viable mechanism for selecting legislators.

Finally, Part Four outlines some strategies and tactics for achieving such a change, and what outcomes might be expected.

Democracy has mutated many times, and will continue to do so. To make the leap to the next form of democracy we must take a historical run-up, be aware of the contemporary landscape around the take-off point, make sure the leap is possible, and know where we want to land and what we hope to find there. That is what this book sets out to do.

The tantalising possibility that we can govern ourselves has presented itself – we no longer need politicians to do it for us. It is time for the end of politicians and for us to become the next wave in the ongoing struggle to demand real democracy, now.

Notes

1. John Keane, *The Life and Death of Democracy* (W. W. Norton, 2009), 308–9, 475.

2. Eric Hobsbawm, *The Age of Revolution: 1789–1848* (Abacus, 1977), 136.

3. Jacques-Guillaume Thouret, *Report on the Basis of Political Eligibility* (1789), from https://chnm.gmu.edu/revolution/d/282/.

4. William Doyle, *The Oxford History of the French Revolution* (Oxford University Press, 1989), 124, 318–19, 420; Josep M. Colomer, *Political Institutions: Democracy and Social Choice* (Oxford University Press, 2001), 54–6.

5. Keane, *Democracy*, 249, highlights how tax and representation were commonly linked centuries before the American Civil War.

6. Colomer, *Political Institutions*, 47, 50–2.

7. http://www.motherjones.com/politics/2014/04/republican-voting-rights-supreme-court-id, http://blogs.reuters.com/great-debate/2013/06/26/gutting-the-landmark-civil-rights-legislation/.

8. Michael Hardt and Antonio Negri, *Commonwealth* (Harvard University Press, 2009), 4.

9. Bernard Manin, *The Principles of Representative Government* (Cambridge University Press, 1997), 102–7.

10. Keane, Democracy, 292 (footnote).

11. Manin, *Principles*, 97; Colomer, *Political Institutions*, 44–50.

12. Keane, *Democracy*, 189.

13. Francis Fukuyama, 'The End of History?' in *The National Interest*, Summer 1989: https://ps321.community.uaf.edu/files/2012/10/Fukuyama-End-of-history-article.pdf.

14. China's constitution was accessed here: http://english.peopledaily.com.cn/constitution/constitution.html; Iran's here: http://www.iranonline.com/iran/iran-info/government/constitution-1.html; and North Korea's here: http://unpan1.un.org/intradoc/groups/public/documents/un-dpadm/unpan045234.pdf.

15. In a *Guardian Weekly* review of Daron Acemoglu and James Robinson's *Why Nations Fail* (Crown Business, 2012), Paul Collier says: 'China has been widely interpreted, especially by African elites, as demonstrating the benefits of autocracy' (13 April 2012).

16. Robert A. Dahl, *On Democracy* (Yale University Press, 1998), 69.

17. Eric Hobsbawm, *The Age of Extremes: The Short Twentieth Century 1914–1991* (Abacus, 1995), 58; and Keane, *Democracy*, 889, note 7, for recent instances of dictators claiming to be ruling democratically.

18. Anthony King, *Who Governs Britain?* (Pelican, 2015), 76; Keane, *Democracy*, 758; and, for example, http://www.ipsos-mori.com/researchpublications/researcharchive/2818/Doctors-are-most-trusted-profession-politicians-least-trusted.aspx; http://www.ipsos-mori.com/Assets/Docs/Polls/Veracity2011.pdf; http://www.edelman.com/insights/intellectual-property/2014-edelman-trust-barometer/; http://www.theguardian.com/world/2011/mar/13/guardian-icm-europe-poll-2011.

19. http://edition.cnn.com/2014/11/04/politics/midterm-exit-polls-1/.

20. King, *Britain*, 77.

21. King, *Britain*, 39.

22. Stuart Wilks-Heeg, Andrew Blick and Stephen Crone, *How Democratic is the UK? The 2012 Audit* (Executive Summary), 13, 16, 17: https://democraticaudituk.files.wordpress.com/2013/06/exec-summary.pdf; see also Paul F. Whiteley, 'Is the Party Over? The Decline of Party Activism and Membership Across the Democratic World', *Party Politics*, 2011, Vol. 17, No. 1, 21–44; Keane, *Democracy*, 753–4.

23. Barack Obama, https://twitter.com/potus/status/684158987185614849.

24. 'Embassy Posts go to Obama's Big Donors', *Guardian Weekly*, 19 July 2013; and 'Obama Ambassadors Court Controversy', *Guardian Weekly*, 21 January 2014.

25. Keane, *Democracy*, 841.

26. Russell Dalton, *Democratic Challenges, Democratic Choices: The Erosion of Political Support in Advanced Industrial Democracies* (Oxford University Press, 2004), 47.

27. Christopher H. Achen and Larry M. Bartels, *Democracy for Realists: Why Elections Do Not Produce Responsive Government* (Princeton University Press, 2016), 4–6.

28. Keane, *Democracy*, 752.

29. 'Two-fifths of Political Donations Made by Just 76 People', *Guardian Weekly*, 19 June 2015; 'Here is the Real Billion-dollar Question: When will the United States Repair its Damaged Democracy?', *Guardian Weekly*, 9 October 2015.

Part I: Representative Democracy

'Representative democracy as it now is cannot be all for which we can reasonably hope.'

—John Dunn, *Democracy: A History*

Chapter 1: Counting Democracies

Democracy is a chameleon. To win the struggle to become the leading ideal of the source of political legitimacy throughout much of the world (and all of the 'free world'[1]) it has changed its colours dramatically against each social, cultural and economic backdrop within which it has emerged. Though perhaps 'chameleon' is too generous a word; its numerous mutations have spread so successfully that 'virus' or 'parasite' may be more appropriate.

There is little, if any, recognisably continuous tradition connecting the 'rule by the people' of the relatively short-lived (a few hundred years) democracy in the city state of Athens in ancient Greece to the surprising reincarnation of democracy in the 19th century – more than 2,000 years later – in the aftermath of the three great revolutions that were the harbingers of the modern era: the Glorious Revolution in England (1688), the American Revolution (1763–83) and the French Revolution (1789–99).[2]

Measuring this modern resurgence of democracy is a fraught affair. Any attempt to count democracies requires both a clear definition of what constitutes a democracy and an objective ability to measure a state against any such definition. Both the defining and the measuring are areas of contestation and contention.

Philosophers and political scientists have probably disputed the definition of democracy ever since the word was first used, although there is little doubt it stems from two basic principles: political equality among adult citizens and popular control of the institutions of government.[3] However, this merely shifts the locus of debate, for what these two principles entail are further conundrums.

Political equality is intuitively defined as every adult counting for one, and no adult for more than one. The simplicity is deceptive. Depending on the electoral system (and the citizenship laws), it is obvious that the votes of any permanent minorities (if they *can* vote) may count for nothing if their preferred candidate is never elected. Their voices may never be represented. The debate between plurality majority (first-past-the-post or winner-takes-all) and proportional forms of representation in electoral systems hinges on this dilemma. In plurality-majority voting systems, such as that of the UK, one candidate is elected from each area, resulting in a parliament typically dominated by two leading parties. In such systems, political equality refers to an equality of initial *opportunity* to vote. In proportional voting systems, as used, for example, in the Netherlands, multiple politicians are usually elected from extended areas in proportion to the votes gained (which often results in many parliamentary parties, and hence coalition governments). The equality in proportional systems refers to the equality of influence on the *outcome*. In both systems, each vote has an equal value in *theory*, although in plurality-majority systems it is obvious that many more votes will have no value in *practice*, as they will not contribute to the composition of parliament. The analysis of the political inequality of certain votes could go even further: election results in UK-type systems often hinge on the outcomes of a handful of marginal seats, so the choices of swinging voters in these seats may be crucial, making their votes very powerful indeed. Political equality, however easy to define, is notoriously difficult to evaluate.

What about popular control? In ancient Athens, for free male citizens at least, that meant not only turning up to the assembly and voting on proposed legislation, but the possibility of being chosen by lot to serve (for a strictly limited time – rotation of office was important) as a magistrate, in the courts or on the 500-member *boule*, where legislative proposals were drafted. Popular control and equality in Athens also meant an equal probability of being selected to serve in public office.[4] In modern representative democracies, the control is far more distant, and is often framed around concepts of consent to be governed; we give our consent by re-electing the incumbents, or withdraw it by voting them out every few years. However, between elections our options for intervention are far fewer, and this extends especially to the numerous unelected public officials in the governmental bureaucracies. In such an environment, where opportunities to influence outcomes only occur every few years, concepts such as 'accountability' and 'responsive government' and 'tracking the interests of the majority' are deemed very important to any definition of democracy.[5]

It is for these reasons that most observers would insist that democracy requires more than regular, competitive elections that are free and fair. It also requires basic civil liberties, such as freedom of speech and the right to assemble in public, legal constraints on the powers of the rulers and a high degree of media independence.[6]

It should come as no surprise then, when even the definition of democracy is an 'essentially contested concept', that the practical application of these ideals varies considerably, and that every attempt to measure the extent of their application inevitably places countries on a democratic spectrum.[7] This invites the obvious question of where to draw the line between which states are, and which are not, democratic.[8]

'Fortunately,' says Dahl, 'the results tend to agree' about differing criteria for how to define and measure a democracy.[9] However, in presenting the graph in Figure 1 it should be remembered that alternative metrics exist that will produce marginally different results. The Polity IV index is one measure of the democratic level of a nation. It is hosted by George Mason University in the US and ranges between –10 for strongly autocratic regimes and 10 for consolidated democracies.[10] Figure 1 shows the count of countries with an index of six and above (both weak and strongly democratic countries), and those with eight or above (only strongly democratic countries), displaying a clear dip during World War II, and a swift increase after the 'velvet' revolutions around 1989 that accompanied the collapse of Soviet communism.

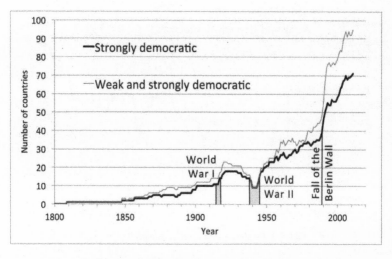

Figure 1: Number of democratic countries over time.

There are many caveats to reading this graph as clear evidence of the triumph of democracy. Universal adult suffrage, perhaps the most commonly understood minimum component of modern representative democracy, only became commonplace after 1915 – in the US after 1919, in the UK in 1928 and in France in 1944 – so it could be reasonably argued that the count should actually be zero before New Zealand introduced women's suffrage in 1893, only rising to five in

1915.[11] Indeed, the US appears as our first 'democracy' in Figure 1 when property qualifications on the right to vote were mostly abolished (for white men only) in the early 1800s.

Furthermore, the relatively steady increase in democracies since the end of World War II ignores the accompanying explosion in the number of nation states resulting from successful struggles against colonialism in the decades after the war, and the collapse and disintegration of the USSR after 1989. The more meaningful percentage of nations (ignoring several difficulties with defining what a nation is, and excluding micro-states of fewer than half a million people) scoring highly on the Polity IV scale is shown in Figure 2.[12] Yet even this ignores the large differences in population size of the various nation states. Figure 3 is the global proportion of people living under democratic regimes from 1950 onwards.

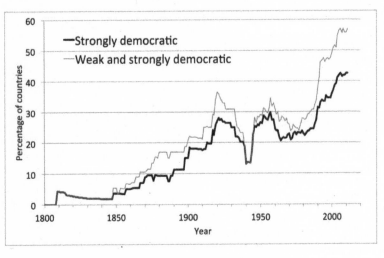

Figure 2: Percentage of democratic countries over time.

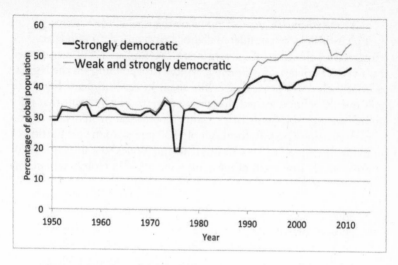

Figure 3: Percentage of global population in a democratic country over time.

The period between the end of World War II and the fall of the Berlin Wall in 1989 was a remarkably stable one, during which approximately one-third of humanity lived in a democracy – the significant dip around 1975 is when Indira Gandhi's government of the most populous democracy, India, declared a state of emergency, suspended basic civil liberties, postponed elections and detained or arrested thousands of political opponents. During this troubled time, the Polity Index of the country dropped to seven.

Only in the last few decades have more or less half the people of the planet lived in a democracy, depending on how stringently democracy is defined. It can, perhaps, tentatively be claimed that the default governance structure of new nations – and nations newly liberated from autocracy – has finally become democracy.

These graphs, however, serve only as an entry point to the history of modern democracy; we should not invest too much faith in the actual details. They offer a framework around which a narrative of waves, setbacks and eventual triumph has been constructed.[13]

The 'first wave' designates the gradual appearance of constitutional parliamentarianism that struggled to take root in the aftermath of the various cycles of revolution and counter-revolution throughout the late 18th and 19th centuries. In the 100 years after the French Revolution, for example, the country fluctuated between monarchy, empire and republic, each often punctuated by fierce bouts of revolution, uprising and bloodshed.[14]

As noted above, almost none of the elected assemblies of this first phase would be considered democratic by modern standards. The Congress of the first US government, meeting in 1789, was elected by a very restricted constituency, typically (depending on the legislation of each state) propertied white men. In revolutionary France, it was openly acknowledged that property restrictions meant that only approximately one-sixth of the adult population would be enfranchised. Britain's Great Reform Act of 1832 increased the proportion of individuals entitled to vote in England and Wales to a similar level of approximately one-sixth of the adult population.[15] Hobsbawm points out:

> The ruling class of [1830–80] was to be the 'grande bourgeoisie' of bankers, big industrialists and sometimes top civil servants, accepted by an aristocracy which effaced itself or agreed to promote primarily bourgeois policies, unchallenged as yet by universal suffrage... Its political system [was] liberal institutions safeguarded against democracy by property or educational qualifications for the voters... In the USA, however, Jacksonian democracy marks a step beyond this [by] the defeat of the non-democratic propertied oligarchs whose role corresponded to what was now triumphing in Western Europe...[16]

This first wave of democracy also contained blatant contradictions regarding equality when applied to non-whites. "'Race'... penetrated the ideology of the period almost as deeply as "progress'", says Hobsbawm. As the economic and military supremacy of the capitalist countries was systematically translated into colonial expansion, annexation and the rise of empires and 'spheres of influence', no one considered any 'subjects' of the newly dominated lands to be citizens fit for inclusion in a democracy.[17]

Yet, at least in the West, a minimally popular form of government with a slowly increasing franchise was provoking less anxiety among the ruling classes. This initial spread of democracy did not last, however, its growth peaking in the 1920s before declining steadily in the following two decades. Two world wars, communist revolution in Russia in 1917, the Great Depression throughout the 1930s and early 1940s, and the rise of fascism and a resurgent barbarism destroyed the ideals and hopes of the Enlightenment embodied by classical liberalism and the tentative democratic flowering. The number of functioning democracies collapsed, and to most observers 'the world trend seemed clear'; across the globe democracy was in retreat and, according to Hobsbawm, appeared all but doomed by the end of World War II.[18]

The failure of democracies became a common feature throughout the 20th century, and continues to be so in the present. 'On more than seventy occasions democracy collapsed and gave way to an authoritarian regime', and with so many fatalities it is understandable that 'nobody seriously predicted or expected its post-war renaissance'.[19] Since World War II, many forward surges of democracy have continued to be trampled quickly and overthrown by dictators. As Keane is at pains to point out, there is no real pattern in the progress or retreat of democracy; it 'dwells in the house of contingency', where often undemocratic forces are the cause of the spread of democracy. No wonder that the more recent democratic waves (the Rose Revolution in Georgia in 2003, the Orange Revolution in Ukraine in 2004–5 and the Arab Spring from 2010) again surprised everybody.[20]

So how is it, some three or four generations after the end of World War II, that liberal democracy now describes our ideal of how to govern a nation, and is by some, like Fukuyama, proclaimed the end point of history? How did liberal democracy come to win the ideological battle against monarchy, aristocracy and dictatorship, so that the 20th century can now be referred to as 'democracy's century' and 'an era of unparalleled triumph'?[21] Why are we so ambivalently attached to this form of governance – loathing politicians, lobbyists and their ilk, yet horrified at the thought of the still-common alternatives of single-party dictatorship or military junta?

It is far easier to document *what* happened than to determine *why* it happened. Many people have tried to answer the latter question, and the inherent difficulties and controversial nature of historical analysis should not be doubted. With this caveat in mind, the next chapter attempts to trace the roots and sporadic growth of democracy to enable us to better appreciate the remarkable domination of this idea. A clearer understanding of the origins of the problems of modern representative democracy will then provide inspiration for potential solutions.

Notes

1. See Freedom House, and its regular reports on the state of democracy – for example, *Freedom in the World 2012 Report*, http://www.freedomhouse.org/sites/default/files/FIW 2012 Booklet_0.pdf. It should be pointed out that less than half the nations of the world (comprising less than half the global population) were rated as 'free' in this report.

2. But see Keane, *Democracy*, 78–272, who spends nearly 200 pages following the narrow and twisting trail of power-sharing assemblies into Europe and out into the Muslim world and then back into Europe again, through the Church's struggles and structures, to the appearance of parliaments in the Iberian Peninsula and later 'aristocratic democracy' in the Netherlands and Poland in the 15th century.

3. Keane, *Democracy*, 861: 'It goes without saying that the principle of the equality of people has always been fundamental to the democratic ideal', although see also 687: 'single-minded, a priori definitions of democracy lost their meaning [after 1945]'.

4. Manin, *Principles*, 11–12, 29–31. Not that the Athenians of the time would have thought in terms of probabilities.

5. For definitions of democracy, see: Anne Phillips, *The Politics of Presence* (Oxford University Press, 1995), 27, 30–1; Dahl, *Democracy*, 37–8; Keane, *Democracy*, 166, 553–4; and for a conception 'against the conventional view', see Clarissa Rile Hayward, 'Making Interest: On Representation and Democratic Legitimacy,' in Ian Shapiro, Susan C. Stokes, Elizabeth J. Wood and Alexander S. Kirchner (eds), *Political Representation* (Cambridge University Press, 2009), 111–35; and that the purpose of government is to 'multiply and challenge governmental claims to represent the people', in Bryan Garsten, 'Representative Government and Popular Sovereignty' in Shapiro *et al.* (eds), *Representation*, 91. Note that the claim that democracies ensure the equal right to stand for office is often unfounded; for example, in the US, citizens under 30 years of age do not have the right to stand for many offices, such as president, and the courts, when challenged, have denied that standing for office is a democratic right.

6. Dahl, *Democracy*, Chapter Four. Freedom House's *Freedom in the World 2012 Report* says freedom entails far more than universal suffrage; a free country 'is one where there is open political competition, a climate of respect for civil liberties, significant independent civic life, and independent media' (http://www.freedomhouse.org/sites/default/files/FIW 2012 Booklet_0.pdf).

7. John S. Dryzek with Simon Niemeyer, *Foundations and Frontiers of Deliberative Governance* (Oxford University Press, 2010), 21. The 'continued dispute over the key components of what democracy means is actually integral to the very idea of democracy itself'.

8. For a list of works that attempt this, including work by Michael Coppedge and Wolfgang H. Reinicke, Freedom House, and the polity database, see Dahl, *Democracy*, Appendix C, 'On Counting Democratic Countries'. The Economist Intelligence Unit (https://www.eiu.com/) also publishes a regular Democracy Index.

9. Dahl, *Democracy*, 197.

10. This data is taken from http://www.systemicpeace.org/inscr/inscr.htm (specifically the file http://www.systemicpeace.org/inscr/p4v2011.xls). The population data used for Figure 3 is from the International Database of the US

Bureau of Census (http://www.census.gov/population/international/data/idb/).

11. Various sub-national entities introduced some minimal franchise of women before this, but here we restrict ourselves to elections to national assemblies of nation states. Note that in New Zealand women could not stand for parliament at this time, so an alternate starting date for full suffrage is Finland in 1906. In the UK, some propertied women achieved the right to vote in 1918, but equality with men was only granted in 1928. It can also be convincingly argued that universal adult suffrage only occurred in the US in 1965 (after the Civil Rights Act of 1964), and in Switzerland it did not occur until 1971. National suffrage rights for all non-citizen permanent residents remain exceptionally rare, with New Zealand since 1975 being a notable exception, although in the EU, suffrage for EU and local elections for non-citizen permanent residents exists. If legitimacy is indeed based on the ideal that every permanent resident of a place obligated by the laws of that place should have input into who formulates those laws, then why are many, such as immigrants, still excluded from this right?

12. Eric Hobsbawn, *The Age of Empire: 1875–1914* (Abacus, 1994), 23.

13. Samuel P. Huntington, *The Third Wave: Democratization in the Late Twentieth Century* (University of Oklahoma Press, 1991); see also Keane, *Democracy*, 671–5, for an outline and strong criticism of this narrative.

14. Hobsbawm, *Revolution*, 136.

15. Keane, *Democracy*, 503–4; Colomer, *Political Institutions*, 44–54.

16. Hobsbawm, *Revolution*, 140.

17. Keane, *Democracy*, 367 and 378; Hobsbawm, *Empire*, 32, 57–8.

18. Hobsbawm, *Extremes*, Chapter Four, particularly 109–12, 135–6.

19. Dahl, *Democracy*, 145; Hobsbawm, *Extremes*, 141.

20. Keane, *Democracy*, 653–4; 161, 674; and 659: 'the rejuvenation of democracy [in Latin America in the 1980s] came as a grand surprise to almost everyone'. In 2010, just before the outbreak of democratic struggles across significant parts of North Africa and the Middle East, the Economist Intelligence Unit published the report *Democracy in Retreat* (http://www.eiu.com).

21. Freedom House, Inc., *Democracy's Century: A Survey of Global Political Change in the 20th Century* (2003); Dahl, *Democracy*, 180.

Chapter 2: The Slow Emergence

The word 'democracy' comes from the ancient Greek noun *demokratia*, which means 'rule by the people', although no one today could seriously claim that 'the people' make the rules in any modern nation state that calls itself democratic. In Joseph Schumpeter's words: 'Democracy does not mean and cannot mean that the people actually rule in any obvious sense of the terms "people" and "rule." Democracy means only that the people have the opportunity of accepting or refusing the men [*sic*] who are to rule them.'[1] We are ruled by our elected politicians. Every few years they must do no worse than other politicians vying for our vote, or at least the votes of those in our societies who care enough and are enfranchised to give them.

The chronicle of people in positions of power using assemblies as a peaceful mechanism for legislating stretches back to earliest recorded history. Evidence from Mesopotamia-Syria, where writing first originated, of the occurrence of assemblies dates from the second and third millennia BCE. By 1500 BCE, assemblies were common on the Indian subcontinent. In myths from the Mesopotamian region, assemblies of gods deciding the fates of people and places date from similar times, and are also commonplace in later ancient Greek myths – stories that attest to the wide appreciation of the passions and power games among leaders coming together to debate and decide on important matters.[2]

The Athenian assemblies of the fifth and fourth centuries BCE, although they excluded women, slaves and non-citizens, are surely the most famous of the early legislatures. Over 6,000 men regularly came together to debate proposals developed by the randomly selected Council of Five Hundred (the *boule*), each of whom served office for one year only. The Athenians were well aware that what they were doing was remarkable. 'We alone,' said the politician and military commander Pericles, 'regard the man who takes no part in public affairs, not as one who minds his own business, but as good for nothing.'[3] Those men who did prefer private to public life were called *idiotes*, hence our word 'idiot'. An extensive system to fill the vast majority of the public offices used the drawing of lots and strictly limited terms of office to decide who was to be a magistrate and who was to serve in the courts and in the *boule*. Election was reserved for those few positions where narrow, specialist skills were deemed necessary, such as heads of finance and military leaders. However, these were always accompanied by various checks and accountability mechanisms, and anyone could denounce those selected as corrupt or incompetent before the courts. Bernard Manin emphasises that magistrates, the courts and the *boule* possessed real power, such as deciding whether proposals passed by the assembly were lawful. 'Citizens chosen by lot were at the nerve centre of power', says David Van Reybrouck.[4] Juxtaposing Athenian *direct* democracy with modern *representative* democracy is therefore too simplistic; representatives of the people, usually chosen by lot, filled many hundreds of important positions throughout Athens.[5]

After ancient Athens's demise, assemblies and councils continued to be used by various bodies, particularly by Muslim and Christian institutions, and the appearance of assemblies of representatives in the political sphere can be traced back to at least the 10th century. Assemblies of aristocrats appeared in the Netherlands in 1581 and in Poland in the same century. Typically, they worked to denounce monarchs and either to usurp, or severely constrain, their powers.[6] The practice was even called 'aristocratic democracy', ignoring the apparent oxymoron that equated the *demos* (the ordinary people) with the aristocrats. Although perhaps it was not considered an oxymoron at the time; in 17th-century England, it was still common for the term 'the people' to be used indistinguishably with that of the 'freeholders', i.e., those with sufficient property to be allowed to vote.[7]

Where monarchs survived, it was often alongside parliaments. In 13th-century England, Edward I convened legislative assemblies, but the regular occurrence of parliamentary assemblies was only cemented as an outcome of the English Civil War (1642–51) and the Glorious Revolution (1688). These parliaments were certainly not democratic. As Ellen Meiksins Wood points out: 'It never occurred to Cromwell to claim that what he was proposing was *democracy*. On the contrary, he was deliberately offering a substitute [of constitutional parliament].'[8] The principal participants in the parliaments were often a mix of hereditary lords, church officials and the monarch's advisors. The UK parliament's upper chamber, the House of Lords, is a direct continuation of this tradition.

'Representative government originated not as a democratic practice but as a device by which nondemocratic governments – monarchs, mainly – could lay their hands on precious revenues and other resources they wanted, particularly for fighting wars,' says Dahl. As

Keane observed, they 'often served as political instruments for regulating money supply by consent'.[9] To justify taxing the wealthy, monarchs were compelled to give them a voice in how their money was spent. It was political bargaining among an elite, often either to avoid internal strife or to engage in external conquest. The parliaments were never intended to be, nor to become, democratic.

The British parliamentary system was 'admired in America by the Framers of the Constitution, many of whom hoped to create in America a republic that would retain the virtues of the English system without the vices of a monarchy', says Dahl.[10]

James Madison, one of the key protagonists in the Constitutional Convention that drafted the US constitution in 1787, and later fourth president of the United States, wrote that the republican system he sought entailed *'the total exclusion of the people, in their collective capacity, from any share in the [American governments]'* (emphasis in the original).[11] This is what the convention mostly achieved. Voting for the House of Representatives was in general restricted to wealthy white men, and senators were selected by those rich white men already elected to the state legislatures. It was assumed that the very selectivity of the representative process would guarantee the 'quality of the representative so chosen'. Quality, in this sense, obviously referred to their elite, propertied status and presumed opposition to 'an equal division of property, or… any other improper or wicked project'.[12]

John Adams, first vice-president and second president of the United States, wrote these words:

> Democracy has never been and never can be so durable as aristocracy or monarchy; but while it lasts, it is more bloody than either… Remember, democracy never lasts long. It soon wastes, exhausts and murders itself. There never was a democracy yet that did not commit suicide. It is vain to say that democracy is less proud, less selfish, less ambitious, or less avaricious than aristocracy or monarchy. It is not true, in fact, and nowhere appears in history.[13]

Democracy was, at the time, considered the demon to be avoided.

Manin argues convincingly that the cultured and well-read members of the Constitutional Convention, such as Madison, surely knew that, historically, the longest-lived and most politically effective republics, ancient Rome and Venice, had been ostentatiously aristocratic.[14] Madison (1751–1836) would also have known that key thinkers, from Aristotle to those not so distant from his own time, such as Rousseau (1712–78) and Montesquieu (1689–1755), had consistently linked democratic government with selection by lot, and aristocratic government with selection through election. Aristotle, in *Politics*, states: 'it is thought to be democratic for the offices [of constitutional government] to be assigned by lot, for them to be elected oligarchic'.[15] From Montesquieu we have: 'Selection by lot is in the nature of democracy, selection by choice is in the nature of aristocracy'; and from Rousseau: 'It will be seen why the drawing of lots is more in the nature of democracy... In an aristocracy... voting is appropriate.'[16] It was well understood at the time that elections are aristocratic devices; 'elite' and 'elect', after all, share the same etymological root. Manin surmises that: 'Lot, in [the eyes of Montesquieu and Rousseau], was one of the tried and tested methods of conferring power in a non-hereditary manner.'[17]

Madison explicitly argued that: 'Large [electoral] districts are manifestly favorable to the election of persons of general respectability, and of probable attachment to the rights of property.' His contempt for 'pure democracy' and desire for a constitutional republic where election acts as a 'filter', is in effect an argument for what Michael Hardt and Antonio Negri call an 'elective aristocracy' (as opposed to a hereditary aristocracy) or a 'republic of property'.[18] Madison expected that election throughout a 'vast territory' with a 'substantial population' would produce a government of the most talented and virtuous, which for him was perhaps synonymous with the wealthiest. Some opponents of the proposed Constitution saw this at the time: Samuel Chase (who voted against ratifying the Constitution and later became a Supreme Court judge) said: 'only the gentry, the rich, the well born will be elected'; and Brutus (presumed to be a pseudonym of Robert Yates) stated: 'the natural aristocracy of the country will be elected. Wealth always creates influence.'[19]

As Dunn says:

> The term democracy played no role at all in initiating the crisis of the North American colonies, and no positive role in defining the political structures that brought it to its strikingly durable close. Where it featured at all... it did so most prominently as the familiar name for the negative model, drawn from the experience of Athens, of an outcome which they must at all costs avoid.[20]

Meiksins Wood highlights the specifically Roman, as opposed to Athenian, choice of terms like 'senate', and the Roman eagle as American icon, as obvious appeals to aristocratic republicanism, and not democracy.[21] Keane agrees: 'All the evidence goes against the popular view that [the American revolutionaries] were the "founding fathers" of democracy in their country, or that they were the founders of modern liberal democracy.'[22]

Neither was democracy seen as a key element in the French Revolution until after the fact. The revolution was, at least in part, a struggle to overthrow inherited privilege. It was waged against aristocracy, and for egalitarian virtues. However, even though during and immediately after the revolution the term 'democracy' was employed to motivate and mobilise the masses, almost none of its prominent actors were ever convinced democrats. 'The revolutionaries were from the very beginning split over the issue of whether or not the whole people could participate directly in matters of government, and what that would mean,' says Keane.[23] The franchise of the first constitution was severely restricted by property qualifications justified by the concept of 'active citizenship', as noted above. François-Antoine Boissy d'Anglas, when drawing up the constitution of 1795, argued that: 'We should be governed by the best... [Y]ou will not find such men except among those who, possessing property, are attached to the land that contains it, to the laws that protect it, to the tranquillity that preserves it.'[24] Various mechanisms used throughout the revolutionary period to restrict who was elected included two-tier (indirect) elections, property qualifications to stand as a candidate and restricting voting to those who could read and write.[25] In his newspaper *The People's Friend*, Jean-Paul Marat was already asking in 1790: 'What would we have gained by destroying the aristocracy of birth if it is replaced by an aristocracy of the rich?'[26] Whatever the extent of their democratic commitment, the elites, terrified by what the revolution had unleashed, accepted Napoleon's military dictatorship that ravaged much of Europe, followed by a reluctant return to monarchy.[27]

So how was it that the seed of democracy sprouted in the undemocratic soil of these institutions? In a very real sense, the answer is that it did not: representative democracy was 'a contradiction in terms' to the people of the time.[28] John Adams (the second US president), again, is direct and to the point:

Is not representation an essential and fundamental departure from democracy? Is not every representative government in the universe an aristocracy? Call it despotism; call it oligarchy; call it democracy; call it a mixture ever so complicated; still is it not an aristocracy, in the strictest sense of the word, according to any rational definition of it that can be given?... Representation and democracy are a contradiction in terms.[29]

What did flourish was popular representative government with a franchise that often, but not always, broadened.[30] 'Only in retrospect' did the familiar practice of an elected legislature find itself 'rechristened in the language of the ancient world'.[31] The name 'democracy' stuck, the contradiction was forgotten and the meaning of the term underwent a fundamental redefinition to be associated thereafter with the election of representatives, and much later for those elections to be open to all adults, rich or poor, male or female.

In Britain, as in the US and France, the movement towards universal suffrage was also both gradual and hesitant. It was won neither by ideologues nor by the overthrow of the regime and the sudden proclamation of some democratic utopia, but by the piecemeal, nervous relaxation of exclusivity in the right to vote. Keane portrays the UK's 1832 Reform Act, which 'forced the aristocracy to share power with the new middle classes', as an action whereby 'the Westminster model vaccinated itself against the French disease [of democracy], to stop its spread through the British Isles, by administering a dose of its poison to its own body politic'.[32] The dose was, as all vaccinations should be, quite small.

Certainly, there was struggle and agitation for a widening of the franchise, even as early as the protests of the Diggers and the Levellers around 1650.[33] The Chartist working-class movement of 1838–48 continued the demand, as did the first socialist parties in the 1880s and '90s, to be followed by the suffragettes of New Zealand and Australia (and later the UK and US), and the civil rights movement in the US. Without these important social movements, expanded or universal suffrage would never have remained on the political agenda for so many decades, if not centuries.

Not every radical, and in particular the anarchists, saw universal suffrage as the solution to humanity's woes. Victor Hugo, certainly no radical himself, writing about the Paris rebellion of 1832 in his novel Les Misérables, observed the counter-revolutionary nature of expanding the franchise: 'It is the particular virtue of universal suffrage that it cuts the ground from under the feet of violent revolt and, by giving insurrection the vote, disarms it.'[34]

Rulers, perhaps for this very reason, grudgingly responded to the demands for increased suffrage. However, first 'they had to determine what concessions to the new forces could be made without threatening the social system, or in special cases the political structures, to whose deference they were committed'.[35] Initially, it was a game of strategically conceding some demands for inclusion to dilute the threat of agitation, or to divide a strong and threatening opposition, while maintaining power. Indeed, it is instructive to note that democracy's 'main forward movements... [came] from deft defensive gambits by audacious conservative politicians'.[36] In the UK, Benjamin Disraeli's Reform Act of 1867 was one such example. It almost doubled the franchise (from approximately 10 to 20 per cent of the adult population), though the original proposal contained 'fancy franchises' giving extra votes for graduates, professionals and those with more than £50 in savings. Disraeli described the act both as a 'leap in the dark', and as 'catching the Whigs [the political opposition] bathing and walking off with their clothes'.[37]

Plural voting continued until 1948: 'more than one-tenth of the electorate still had more than one vote on the basis of their property or education qualifications after the 1885 reforms. Between forty and eighty seats in each election were determined by these voters.'[38]

The fear of large extensions of the franchise is intuitively simple to understand. Most observers assumed – and why wouldn't they? – that if universal suffrage was granted and the numerous poor could also vote, then they would rapidly elect their own representatives, obtain power and set about expropriating the wealth of the rich. This was of course why the socialists campaigned so fervently for universal suffrage, and one mystery of modern representative democracy is why this expropriation did not in fact occur.

Perhaps, as the socialists might have said, it did not happen because a 'class consciousness' had not been sufficiently developed among the poor and the workers, or because deference to the upper classes was too strong in the UK. Or is it merely another confirmation of the ancient understanding that elections are essentially aristocratic? Keane describes how the elite of Latin America nonchalantly accepted representative democracy because they 'knew that talk of [rule by] "the best" was just a fancy way of referring to the rich and the powerful'.[39] It was, and still is, the case that 'electioneering was a rich man's pursuit', and voters usually elected people of fame or distinction.[40]

However, the ruling classes did not leave too much to chance. After several more 'prophylactic extensions of the vote… western states had to resign themselves to the inevitable. Democratic politics could no longer be postponed. Henceforth the problem was how to manipulate them.'[41]

Manipulation took many forms. The power of parliaments could be minimised, either through constitutional constraints or by moving as much of the administration of government to bodies of permanently appointed public officials, i.e., the civil service.[42] Or parliament could be supplemented by an unelected (or indirectly elected) second chamber, such as the House of Lords in the UK, or the Senate in the US before 1913. Intimidation, vote-buying and patronage were rife before the use of the secret ballot – 'workers were forced to mark their ballot papers under the watchful eyes of their employers' agents'.[43] Candidates were often expected to transport, house and entertain voters in the run-up to elections in return for their vote. For those suspected of disloyalty, the placement of obstacles to register to vote was commonplace.

In 19th-century Spanish America, 'pact politics', or deal-making between those in power and leaders of prominent social groups able to deliver votes, was 'a new way of governing in the age of representative democracy… [It] was roughly the Spanish American equivalent of the American boss system operated by pork-barrelling parties.'[44]

Political parties sprang up as the franchise expanded. In Europe, workers' parties flourished, but it soon became apparent that the demands of electioneering and the centralised, hierarchical and bureaucratic nature of unions, and other groups federated within such parties, meant ordinary workers would almost never be elected. The book *Political Parties*, written by the sociologist Robert Michels in 1911, was one of the first to claim that elite rule in *any* party system was inevitable.[45]

As early as 1850, political parties in the US operated a ubiquitous system of patronage and spoils for their members. 'Voluntary' contributions to the principal parties were required to get on electoral tickets, and federal jobs and sinecures were dished out by the winners, with three per cent of the resulting salary often required to be returned to the party. Barrels of money oiled these political machines operating a 'patronage system that resembled a duopoly in the business world'.[46] Party politics emerged hand in hand with pervasive political corruption; from the moment most men were given the right to vote it became impossible for anyone without wealth and pow-

erful connections to enter politics. 'Quite a few observers noted...
the deadly mix of democracy and dollars.' Even though the US 'gave
birth, for the first time anywhere in the world, to full-time [political]
parties and full-time politicians', its immediate effect was, as some
contemporaries protested, that 'the corruption of the ballot has ren-
dered our elections little less than a disgraceful farce'.[47]

It was around this time, several decades after the American Revolution, that US citizens first came to call their form of government
a democracy, and forgot their previous dislike of the term. This
occurred especially after the publication of Alexis de Tocqueville's
influential *Democracy in America* in 1835 and 1840, when the etymological gymnastics were adopted with enthusiasm. Soon, democracy
was even being used to justify war – for example, in the Mexican-
American war of 1846–48 that ended with the US in control of a large
swathe of southern land, including all of modern-day Texas.[48] 'As the
nineteenth century wore on, talk of democratic right, backed by the
threatened or actual use of force, became commonplace', culminating
in President Wilson arguing that the US must enter into World War
I since: 'The world must be made safe for democracy.'[49]

As the US expanded its territory in the 19th century, France
continued to be convulsed by bouts of revolution and reaction. A
four-year-long Second Republic emerged after the 1848 revolution,
including 'the first mass election in contemporary history' with perhaps 10 million eligible male voters, but it was only in 1870 that the
Third Republic initiated, more or less, the period of permanent, if
minimal, representative democracy.[50]

Eventually, improvements were made to the legitimacy of representative democracy: the 'Australian' secret ballot was introduced,
direct election of most politicians was made law (in the US in 1913),
exams for entry into the civil service were introduced, public disclo-
sure laws for politicians mandated and the franchise extended to most
adult men, at least in theory.[51]

Overt corruption gave way to more subtle forms of persuasion
– it is no coincidence that nationalism blossomed in this era. 'We
are now so used to an ethnic-linguistic definition of nations that
we forget that this was, essentially, invented in the later nineteenth
century.'[52] Suddenly monarchs appeared dressed in some fictional
national dress. Processions and flag-waving (and near worship in the
US) became a sport on the newly proclaimed national holidays, such
as Empire Day in Britain, instituted in 1902.[53] Monuments to glo-
ries past were erected, and national anthems adopted and sung with

gusto at military parades and especially in the rapidly expanding state primary school system, where linguistic purity was often imposed: 'Until the triumph of television, there was no medium of secular propaganda to compare with the classroom.'[54] Universal military service, with strong nationalistic overtones, picked up where education finished, and it was adopted across much of Europe. With the rise of working-class parties and universal suffrage, the state *needed* to make the nation: 'Authorities in an increasingly democratic age... needed a way of welding together the state's subjects against subversion and dissidence. "The nation" was the new civic religion of states. It provided... a counterweight to those who appealed to other loyalties over state loyalty... perhaps above all to class.'[55] To the challenge of socialist class-consciousness, the rulers responded with patriotism. That it was effective is shown clearly by the exultant rush to arms by the people at the outbreak of World War I; that it could also be dangerous was shown by the rise of Nazism and fascism a few decades later.[56]

The slow extension of suffrage to all men, and the beginning of that extension to women, introduced 'the era of public political hypocrisy, or rather duplicity, and hence also that of political satire... For what intelligent observer could overlook the yawning gap between public discourse and political reality.'[57] The new breed of professional politicians could no longer be brutally sincere, for 'what candidate wanted to tell his voters that he considered them too stupid and ignorant to know what was best in politics... No longer would the expected implications of democracy be discussed... with the frankness and realism of... 1867... [T]he men who governed wrapped themselves in rhetoric.'[58]

The era of large public election campaigns developed alongside, and sometimes hand in hand with, the increasing sophistication of advertising, propaganda and mass media, initially in the form of popular newspapers. This was a mere taste of things to come: with the invention of radio and television, the popular media would fundamentally transform and dominate politics. Bruce Bimber, in *Information and American Democracy*, details three periods of democratic evolution related to changes in communications technologies, beginning with the invention of the US Postal Service and the growth of the newspaper industry.[59]

Then came the crisis years of 1914–44. After the Russian Revolution of 1917–18 (and the wave of unrest that followed in Europe and across the world), and the implicit threat to private property that communism theoretically contained, democracy was rapidly ejected and dismissively ignored by nearly all who had the power to do so. Rulers, by their actions, showed that they continued to hold democracy in contempt. 'In 1918–20 legislative assemblies were dissolved or became ineffective in two European states, in the 1920s in six, the 1930s in nine, while German occupation destroyed constitutional power in another five during the Second World War.'[60]

The palpable fear of social revolution before and especially during the Great Depression led to fascism and dictatorship in Germany, Italy and Spain. What Hitler, Mussolini and Franco performed in Europe, military coup performed in Latin America. The de-democratisation of nation states surged.[61] Earlier, democracy may have been a convenient gamble to legitimise power, but when the basic consensus required by democracy to bargain for compromise was undermined by unemployment and food shortages, the wealthy and better off were once again insecure before the hydra of the masses. The 'hell of social strife and political despotism... very nearly reduced representative democracy to the bones of an extinct political species', says Keane.[62] There was little hesitation in seizing power, and little support for those attempting to defend democracy. When Franco threatened and overthrew Spanish democracy in 1936–39, Winston Churchill could not bring himself to support the republicans.[63]

Democracies collapsed, or were overthrown, across the globe. According to the Polity IV index (see Figure 1) there were only nine democracies remaining in the midst of war. The 'great flame of democracy' needed to be bravely shielded 'from the blackout of barbarism', as President Roosevelt put it in 1941.[64]

Somehow, democracy survived, and even thrived in the years after World War II. Almost nowhere within democratic nation states today are voices heard other than for the continued support and promotion of democracy, at least within their own borders, and often outside of them. The fact that two of the three major victors were democracies is not enough to explain the remarkable turnaround in democracy's fortunes. Few people at the end of the war foresaw its stunning post-war success, and more than a few actively celebrated what they thought was its imminent demise.[65]

Notes

1. Joseph A. Schumpeter, *Capitalism, Socialism and Democracy*, sixth edition (Unwin, 1987), 284–5.

2. Keane, *Democracy*, 90–5, 111–24. These assemblies were in no way democratic, of course; the people had virtually no say whatsoever.

3. Keane, *Democracy*, 45; and quote attributed to Pericles on 66.

4. David Van Reybrouck, *Against Elections: The Case for Democracy* (Bodley Head, 2016), 64.

5. Manin, *Principles*, 8, 15, 17–18, 22, 25.

6. Keane, *Democracy*, 153: 'Muslims effectively built a political bridge that linked the ancient assemblies of Syria-Mesopotamia, Phoenicia and Greece with the coming world of representative democracy.' See also 170: 'The first parliament was born of despair' at the seemingly invincible advance of Muslims into Europe via southern Spain. The role of Christian institutions is detailed on 207, 218, 221, 226–7, including this: 'Without Jesus, there would have been no representative government, or representative democracy.' On the Netherlands and Poland, see 242, 257, 467–9: the Dutch philosopher Spinoza (1632–77) was one of the first modern writers to use the term 'democracy' in a positive light.

7. Hardt and Negri, *Commonwealth*, 51.

8. Ellen Meiksins Wood, *Democracy against Capitalism: Renewing Historical Materialism* (Cambridge University Press, 1995), 231.

9. Dahl, *Democracy*, 103; Keane, *Democracy*, 184. The undemocratic nature of these parliaments is highlighted on 181–2, 184, 187.

10. Dahl, *Democracy*, 21.

11. Madison quoted in Dunn, *Democracy*, 74–5, 79 (original 'exclusion' quote can be found here: http://press-pubs.uchicago.edu/founders/documents/v1ch4s27.html or http://en.wikisource.org/wiki/The_Federalist_(Dawson)/62).

12. Madison quoted in Dunn, *Democracy*, 78.

13. Charles Francis Adams, *The Works of John Adams, Second President of the United States*, Volume 6 (Boston, 1851), 483–4.

14. See Dunn, *Democracy*, 120, regarding 'ostentatiously aristocratic'; and Manin, *Principles*, 1: 'Rousseau saw an immense gulf between a free people making its own laws and a people electing representatives to make laws for it'; and 4: 'In the late eighteenth century, then, a government organized along representative lines was seen as differing radically from democracy'; and 44: 'the presence of these considerations in the works of authors whose influence is beyond doubt shows that the contrast between the two methods of appointment [lot and election] retained a measure of importance in the political culture of the seventeenth and eighteenth centuries... The cultivated elites that established representative government were certainly aware of them'; and see also 63, 79.

15. Aristotle quoted in Manin, *Principles*, on 43. For the original, see Aristotle, *Politics*, 1294b – for example, http://www.perseus.tufts.edu/hopper/text?doc=Perseus:text:1999.01.0058:book=4:section=1294b.

16. Montesquieu and Rousseau are quoted in Manin, *Principles*, 70, 74, 77.

17. Manin, *Principles*, 43.

18. Madison quoted in Manin, *Principles*, 123; Michael Hardt and Antonio Negri, *Multitude: War and Democracy in the Age of Empire* (Penguin, 2005), 244–5; and Hardt and Negri, *Commonwealth*, 4–20.

19. Quoted in Manin, *Principles*, 109–10, 113.

20. Dunn, *Democracy*, 72; see also Keane, *Democracy*, 83–4.

21. Meiksins Wood, *Democracy*, 225.

22. Keane, *Democracy*, 83; see also 163, 275–7, 200–3, 290.

23. Keane, *Democracy*, 477.

24. Quoted in Andrew Jainchill, *Reimagining Politics After the Terror: The Republican Origins of French Liberalism* (Cornell University Press, 2008), 43.

25. Manin, *Principles*, 98, 100; Colomer, *Political Institutions*, 54.

26. Michel Vovelle, *The Fall of the French Monarchy 1787–1792* (Cambridge University Press, 1984) 208; see also http://www.open.edu/openlearn/ocw/mod/oucontent/view.php?printable=1&id=1683.

27. Dunn, *Democracy*, 92, 97, 101.

28. Dahl, *Democracy*, 94; and Meiksins Wood, *Democracy*, 216–17.

29. Adams, *The Works of John Adams*, vol. 6, 462.

30. Keane, *Democracy*, 168, 410–11 lists several examples where the franchise narrowed, and argues against any notion of a Law of Evolutionary Expansion of the Franchise.

31. Dunn, *Democracy*, 72.

32. Keane, *Democracy*, 503–4 and 554–5.

33. Hardt and Negri, *Commonwealth*, 40, 45, 51.

34. Anarchists: Dunn, *Democracy*, 153–4. Emma Goldman's essay 'Woman Suffrage' in *Anarchism and Other Essays* (1917) also states: 'Are we to assume that the poison already inherent in politics will be decreased, if women were to enter the political arena?... Is woman [in places where she can vote] no longer considered a mere sex commodity?'; Victor Hugo, *Les Misérables* (Penguin, 1862, translated by Norman Denny 1982), 890.

35. Eric Hobsbawm, *The Age of Capital: 1848–1875* (Abacus, 1997), 91.

36. Dunn, *Democracy*, 154.

37. Hobsbawm, *Empire*, 86; and Hobsbawm, *Capital*, 90–3.

38. Colomer, *Political Institutions*, 49. The 1884 and '85 Acts extended the geographical reach of the Reform Act of 1867.

39. Keane, *Democracy*, 393–4.

40. Manin, *Principles*, 97, 130.

41. Hobsbawm, *Empire*, 86.

42. Hobsbawm, *Extremes*, 139.

43. Keane, *Democracy*, 753.

44. Keane, *Democracy*, 407.

45. Referred to in Manin, *Principles*, 206–8.

46. Keane, *Democracy*, 294–302, 327–41.

47. Keane, *Democracy*, 298.

48. Keane, *Democracy*, 369–71.

49. Keane, *Democracy*, 371, 375, 805–7. Echoes of this justification for war can still be heard today – for example, George W. Bush's ex post facto portrayal of the war in Iraq (after 'weapons of mass destruction' were not found) as part of a 'global democratic revolution' (http://www.washingtonpost.com/wp-dyn/articles/A7991-2003Nov6.html). Many (typically western) commentators also claimed that the 'Arab Spring' revolutions of 2010 onwards were driven by the demand for democracy. However, the popular cry on the streets of Egypt was firstly for bread. Similar claims were made at the time of the disintegration of the USSR, although a case can be made that hunger had much to do with it – for example, Hobsbawm, *Extremes*, 492: 'Hunger and shortage lie behind everything that happened in the last two years of the USSR.'

50. Colomer, *Political Institutions*, 54.

51. See Keane, *Democracy*, 524–9, on the secret ballot, but see 913, note 35: sometimes the secret ballot made vote-buying even easier! The arrival of 'Progressivism' and various mechanisms to clean up politics is detailed in 345–7 and 354–6.

52. Hobsbawm, *Empire*, 146, but see also 105-7, 148.

53. Keane, *Democracy*, 771.

54. Hobsbawm, *Empire*, 150.

55. Hobsbawm, *Empire*, 149.

56. See also Keane, *Democracy*, 558–65, on the rise of nation states and nationalism, and 569 on its undermining of democracy: 'the deadliest forces were nationalism'.

57. Hobsbawm, *Empire*, 88.

58. Hobsbawm, *Empire*, 87–8.

59. Bruce Bimber, *Information and American Democracy: Technology in the Evolution of Political Power* (Cambridge University Press, 2003).

60. Hobsbawm, *Extremes*, 111.

61. Keane, *Democracy*, 451–4, 573–8.

62. Keane, *Democracy*, 457, 567–72.

63. Hobsbawm, *Extremes*, 110, 113, 127, 135, 138, 141. That our rulers continued to hold democracy largely in contempt was made obvious by the repeated overthrow (direct or via proxies) of 'unfriendly' democracies such as in Iran in 1953 and Chile in 1973 by the US and its allies (Dahl, *Democracy*, 57–8). The audible nervousness with which the 2012 election of members of the Muslim Brotherhood in Egypt was greeted, and the acquiescence in their subsequent overthrow, and the outright rejection of the 2006 democratic win by Hamas in Palestine, attests to the realpolitik whereby the desire for allies and stability often trumps that of democracy.

64. Keane, *Democracy*, 729.

65. Keane, *Democracy*, 570–4, and 659 on the 'grand surprise' of the rejuvenation of democracy (in Latin America).

Chapter 3: An Unexpected Revival

Two of the most notable political and economic features of the decades directly after World War II were the rise and domination of the mass-produced items of consumer-driven capitalism and the anti-communist Cold War struggles. That every democratic nation is also capitalist (but not vice versa), and that many democracies were united in their ideological battle against communism (very few *explicit* wars have occurred *between* democratic states[1]), were recognised at the time and immediately seized upon to postulate that there is a natural affinity between democracy and capitalism.

Friedrich Hayek, in *The Road to Serfdom*, claimed that the US had 'progressively abandoned that freedom in economic affairs without which personal and political freedom has never existed in the past. Although... socialism means slavery, we have steadily moved in the direction of socialism.'[2] The book became famous for claiming an inevitable link between centralised (socialist) planning and totalitarian dictatorship, postulating that economic freedom is a prerequisite for personal and political freedoms.

In *Rationalizing Capitalist Democracy*, S. M. Amadae traces the development of rational choice theory (also called public choice theory), which forms an intellectual basis for the linking of capitalism and democracy, from Hayek to other academics such as Kenneth Arrow, James Buchanan, Joseph Schumpeter, Anthony Downs and Karl Popper. The tradition was continued by Milton Friedman, in particular with his book *Capitalism and Freedom*, published in 1962.[3] In the US in particular, says Amadae, rational choice theory strove to recast democratic choice in the same terms as market choice: politicians were the products competing for people's votes, and voting itself was seen as an act of consumption. To understand the relationship between capitalism and democracy, the proponents of rational choice refashioned 'democratic theory into an individualistic competition that resembles market interactions predicated on self-interest'.[4]

Amadae argues convincingly that rational choice theory was 'from the outset fashioned to render authoritarianism and collectivism theoretically moribund', and provide a solid academic basis for post-war capitalist democracy. To win the perceived struggle of individualism versus authoritarian socialism, the rational choice theorists promulgated the idea that: 'Democracy and *laissez faire* capitalism are united in their dependence on individual freedom', and that 'free market transactions are crucial to an effective democratic society'.[5] Anyone with a totalising view of what is good for society was a power-hungry dictator in disguise; we are all selfish individuals (or 'utility maximisers' in economic jargon) and therefore the only guar- antors of liberal freedoms are democracy in the political sphere and capitalism in the economic sphere.

Amadae describes the impetus for the development of such a the- ory 'as a direct response to American Cold War concerns... in oppo- sition to idealistic democracy, socialist economics, and collectivist sentimentality'.[6] In this reading of the immediate post-war events, linking democracy with capitalism served to defeat the threat of com- munism – or, indeed, the threat of any large-scale government inter- vention in capitalist markets.

Ironically, in the process of delegitimising totalitarian ideologies (all ideologies proclaiming a unitary vision of the good life), rational choice theory also undermined democracy itself. By portraying peo- ple as self-interested, strategic and rational actors (the neoliberal *Homo economicus* concept of humankind) and, moreover, by extending it to politicians, political parties and indeed all government officials, it surely contributed to the widespread cynicism towards politicians and governments of today. Politicians were assumed to be motivated pri- marily by self-interested hunger for power, a political party's principal goal was to win elections and not to enact specific policy initiatives, and the notion that government bureaucracy acts in the public inter- est – or even that there is any such thing as the public interest – was challenged.[7] Much current disaffection with politics has its roots in these ideas, which were originally popularised by rational choice the- orists trying to link democracy with capitalism.

Hayek and his successors, however, faced a dilemma: if people are selfish and there is no such thing as the collective good, who could be trusted to make the decisions about how to manage and distrib- ute collective resources? The solution was to formulate the field of 'rational policy analysis... [which] functioned as a means to relocate the authority for policy decisions from elected officials to a supposedly "objective" technocratic elite'.[8]

The idea has cast a long shadow. In his Reith Lectures in 2009 for the BBC, Michael Sandel inveighs against 'market-mimicking gov- ernance' that includes the 'spurious science' of cost-benefit analysis that 'shifts decision-making from democratic politics to technocrats'.

He sees its appeal as 'a way of making political choices without making hard and controversial moral choices', and posits its beginnings in 'the 1950s and 60s, partly as a reaction against fascist and communist ideologies, and partly as an attempt to spare politics from becoming embroiled in religious strife'.[9] Indeed, during the global financial crisis and subsequent recession that began in 2008, the governments of Greece and Italy were temporarily controlled by so-called 'technocrats' willing to impose austerity. Across Europe in general, austerity was depicted as a technocratic exercise of 'balancing the books', an attempt to depoliticise the ideological belief in small government and the slashing of government programmes, instead of, for example, implementing a wealth or financial transactions tax to raise governmental income.

Rational policy analysis sought to recast policy development and implementation as a management function, guided in broad terms by elected representatives, but whose principal metric for success was economic growth and expansion. Amadae sees this as part of the long-standing 'tendency of elites to develop means to control societal decision-making processes', and the argument that policy is too complex for ordinary people to understand is a direct continuation of this line of thought.[10]

The 'realism' of these men (and they are all men), accompanied by the global rise and domination of the US, provided the necessary theoretical framework for capitalism and democracy's 20th-century triumph; it certainly left an indelible impression regarding the link between the two.

Dahl likens the relationship between democracy and capitalism to a 'tempestuous marriage that is riven by conflict and yet endures because neither partner wishes to separate from the other'.[11] He postulates that 'economic growth is favourable to democracy' and that 'market-capitalism is a powerful solvent of authoritarian regimes' that 'sew [sic] the seeds of their own ultimate destruction' if they develop a dynamic market economy.

After years studying capitalism's historical development, Hobsbawm, unsurprisingly, takes a somewhat contrary view. To him, post-war democracy evolved as the outcome of the secular struggle against social revolution. Democracy, and the New Deal that followed the Great Depression, represented the minimally legitimate form of government that defused the threat of communist revolution while not threatening profits and the private accumulation of wealth. It was obvious then, and still is today, that big business can, and will, operate with any regime that does not expropriate its profits. It appears far more likely that economic growth, if minimally distributed so that the majority of people have enough to eat, lends itself to stability, whatever the type of regime – democratic or totalitarian.[12] When a dog has a bone, it neither bites nor barks.[13] In this view, it is not, as Dahl speculates, capitalist *growth* that produces regime change, but the inevitable inequality and capitalist *crises* that have always periodically punctuated that growth. From the times of poor harvests and food shortages before the French Revolution came Marie Antoinette's (probably apocryphal) reproach to the hungry masses: 'Let them eat cake.'[14] Lenin's promise to the Russian people was for 'Peace, Land and Bread' before the October Revolution. The Arab Spring that began in late 2010 was preceded by rocketing food prices, drought and water shortages, and the first word chanted over and over in protests in Egypt was the Arabic for 'bread' (which can also mean 'livelihood').[15] There is an impressive correlation between high values in the UN Food and Agriculture Organization's Food Price Index and the occurrence of protest, riots and social disruption.[16] An important aspect of many revolutions is economic crises and related food shortages, and not maturing market economies miraculously inducing an accompanying desire for political freedom.

Indeed, Dahl adds the caveat that 'there appears to be no correlation between economic growth and a country's type of government and regime', citing as examples the existence of the many authoritarian capitalist states such as Iran, China and Saudi Arabia.[17] He admits that China will be the greatest test of his theory; will we see democracy blossom in China as its embrace of capitalism advances, or will democracy around the world be displaced by the continued rise and eventual domination of various regimes of authoritarian capitalism?

Keane portrays the democracy that flourished after World War II as a response to 'the devil of unaccountable power' that led to war and the growth of authoritarian and fascist regimes that 'overstepped the mark'.[18] He claims that an essentially new form of democracy – monitory democracy – emerged as an expanding network of civil society groups, using a wide variety of tactics, utilised the power of the greatly enhanced new media (radio, television and print) to successfully promote their interests, monitor politics and politicians, and constrain governments to respect (or implement) fundamental liberties and human rights. This 'post-representative' and 'post-parliamentary' democracy is characterised by a plethora of power-scrutinising mechanisms that strive to keep not only elected representatives and government officials, but also corporations and everyone in positions of power, continuously in check. By doing so, the importance of elections, political parties and legislatures in the political sphere has decreased. The political geography of monitory democracy is described as fundamentally a network structure: 'In the world of monitory democracy, that kind of latticed – viral, networked – pattern is typical, not exceptional.'[19] These network structures are the core topic of Part Two.

The two theses – that democracy flourished by being hitched to capitalism to combat the Cold War on the ideological front, and that it thrived due to a rapid expansion of power-monitoring mechanisms – are not incompatible. The former can provide the post-war theoretical underpinning while the latter details a key component of its recent practical implementation.

Whatever the complex relationship between capitalism, democracy and civil society, there must be little doubt, after democracy's crisis and retreat during 1922–44, that its rising phoenix-like from the ashes of destruction was incalculably aided by the ensuing 'golden years' of capitalism.[20] Peaceful social co-existence is obviously facilitated by prosperity, and having an occasional vote, and a growling pack of democracy watchdogs to highlight corruption, is certainly better than lifelong tyranny and oppression. The two processes of capitalism and democracy have, hand in hand, refashioned each other, softening the edges of the most blatant short-term failures of untrammelled capitalism while refashioning democracy to mean universal suffrage and voting in competitive elections for politicians, generally from the elite of society, who are nonetheless checked in their power by a pervasive civil society.

Taking the long view, democracy is the ancient label adopted for a form of government that is the unintended historical outcome of the 19th-century battle to overthrow the aristocracy and eliminate the bestowing of hereditary privilege.[21] For a while, the powerful learned to adapt the system, or even to use it, so that widening the franchise posed no threat to private property and the continuation of economic inequality. The aristocrats were joined by the wealthy in wielding power.

Although democracy barely survived the years of war and the Great Depression, by the end of the 20th century the conjunction of liberal representative democracy with capitalism (the 'wager on the rich', as Dunn calls it) had definitively won the battle of ideas against authoritarian communism.[22] Democracy persisted because the form of government it came to describe was accepted as the minimally credible authority to rule with the active consent of many, and as it generally selects a subset of the elite to legislate, it is therefore well suited to the current growth-oriented requirements of individualistic capitalism – the 'order of egoism' as Dunn labels it.[23]

Democracy now designates the promise of legal and political equality – following the 'logic of equality', says Dahl – while purposefully ignoring or remaining silent on economic inequality, even though the latter severely undermines or compromises the practical application of the former.[24]

Or would it be more apt to say that, rather than democracy surviving, it mutated? The system perpetuated under the democratic label is perhaps 'an obvious and brazen misnomer'.[25] Its insistence on election as fundamental makes it something that would be unrecognisable to the ancient Athenians and their process of public assemblies and selection of people to important time-limited positions by lot. From the discussion above it is clear that the Founding Fathers of the US would be shocked to hear their constitution called democratic. The word 'democracy' has become a mystification with 'the appearance of inclusion' – nearly every observer acknowledges that the legislative process in democratic countries is one of bargaining among elites with the public occasionally determining which faction of the political elite sits at the high table.[26]

Of course, the accusation that representative democracy is not 'real' democracy in any historical or etymological sense is neither here nor there with regard to its, by now, obvious triumph as the preferred way 'free' societies identify the political organisation of their nation states. In whatever form democracy takes in the future, the remarkably resilient label seems more than likely to persist.

And it is a remarkable outcome. *All* of the citizens, at least in theory, are the equal source of political legitimacy in a democracy. For the first time in history, democracy has become a global language.[27] Whatever we call the system that piggybacked on the postwar economic success of capitalism, we must preface our analysis of its undeniable problems with an appreciation that it has led to several impressively durable and stable nation states accumulating, and concentrating, massive wealth and power where many other states and systems have tried and failed to do so. The freedom to critique its current problems, and conceive of the next step towards a better democracy, only exists because of its past success.

Notes

1. Dahl, *Democracy*, 58; but see Keane, *Democracy*, 796–8, for a scathing critique of this view.

2. Friedrich A. Hayek, *The Road to Serfdom* (University of Chicago Press, 1944), 16.

3. Milton Friedman, *Capitalism and Freedom* (University of Chicago Press, 1962).

4. S. M. Amadae, *Rationalizing Capitalist Democracy: The Cold War Origins of Rational Choice Liberalism* (University of Chicago Press, 2003), 188, quote is from 22.

5. Amadae, *Rationalizing*, 159, 17, 175.

6. Amadae, *Rationalizing*, 155.

7. Amadae, *Rationalizing*, 137, 139, 181.

8. Amadae, *Rationalizing*, 31.

9. Michael Sandel, *A New Citizenship*, Lecture 4: 'A New Politics of the Common Good' (BBC Reith Lecture, 2009). Transcript: http://downloads.bbc.co.uk/rmhttp/radio4/transcripts/20090630_reith.pdf.

10. Amadae, *Rationalizing*, 155.

11. Dahl, *Democracy*, 166, 167, 178.

12. Hobsbawm, *Extremes*, 129, 136–7.

13. Keane, *Democracy*, 412.

14. Even though she probably never said it: http://en.wikipedia.org/wiki/Let_them_eat_cake.

15. http://en.wikipedia.org/wiki/Egyptian_Revolution_of_2011: 'The revolution's main demands chanted over and over in every protest are: Bread [livelihood], Freedom, Social Justice, Human Dignity.' And see, for example, http://www.americanprogress.org/issues/security/report/2013/02/28/54579/the-arab-spring-and-climate-change/.

16. http://necsi.edu/research/social/food_crises.pdf.

17. Dahl, *Democracy*, 170.

18. Keane, *Democracy*, 728–40, 656.

19. Keane, *Democracy*, 688–93, 706, but see 708: 'monitory democracy is [not] mainly or "essentially" a method of taming the power of government'. For the network structure, see 697–9, 745.

20. Hobsbawm, *Extremes*, Chapter Nine; see also Hobsbawm, *Capital*, Chapter Two, to note a similar outcome from 'The Great Boom' of 1848 to the 1870s.

21. Hobsbawm, *Empire*, 181.

22. Dunn, *Democracy*, 160–70, also 186.

23. Dunn, *Democracy*, 160.

24. Dahl, *Democracy*, 10, 158.

25. Dunn, *Democracy*, 155.

26. Amadae, *Rationalizing*, 31.

27. Keane, *Democracy*, 64.

Chapter 4: Democracy's Dilemmas

The problems of modern electoral democracy are many and well documented: large corporations and their armies of lobbyists often exert undue influence on policy; politicians must necessarily develop close ties to the media to manage their brand and spin their side of the story; successful elections need enormous war chests of money, requiring the cultivation of extensive networks of wealthy donors, who are often rewarded with government appointments and, presumably, favourable laws; and the eruption of scandal and the uncovering of overt corruption are depressingly regular. All sides of the political spectrum regularly attack opposition members when these practices slide too far into the realms of questionable or unethical behaviour.

In this chapter, the focus is on two distinct dilemmas: (i) that legislative assemblies in so-called representative democracies are, in various and important ways, highly unrepresentative; and (ii) that politicians and democratic processes are too easily and too often corrupted by money, the media and politicians' desire to remain in power. The structure of regular elections, the distorting effects of political parties and the concentration of wealth and the traditional media into ever fewer hands compromise all democracies. Even if election campaign fundraising and the chasing of high-profile donors is not illegal, the effects of money on access to power justifiably provokes widespread cynicism and disaffection.

What is meant by the word 'representative' in representative democracy is not as simple as it may first appear, as there are multiple meanings and ways for a person to represent other people. Two principal forms of representation are commonly distinguished: *descriptive* and *responsive*.

Descriptive (or indicative, or demographic) representation assumes that the representatives 'should faithfully reproduce significant differences among the population, and reproduce them in proportion to their realization within the community'.[1] In this case, the representatives should be a mirror of the general populace – should in effect form a mini-public – where 'the person [representing me] is my proxy, someone who takes my place, with my authority'.[2] This is still the case in many countries where trial by jury exists. The jury is supposedly a small sample of ordinary people, and the assumption

49

is that they will make the decision that any group of (or even all of) society would have made given the information and time to deliberate on the case. This is participation by proxy: the sample of people participates on behalf of everyone else. Ancient Athens applied the same method, albeit only among free male citizens, to fill their courts and councils. Historically, descriptive representation was the hallmark of democracy; random selection, if a relatively large selection is made from the entire population, can result in those chosen being a reliable sample of the community.

With responsive (or substantive) representation, a representative 'tracks what the representee wants and responds with appropriate action' – they act as delegates or trustees, in theory transmitting the ideas of those they are representing to the assembly.[3] In a very simplistic sense, this is the principle behind how democracy should now work. Modern democracies are legitimate only if the representatives are responsive to the needs and wishes of their constituents. One presumed function of elections is to promote those who listen and respond, and punish those who do not.

In *The Politics of Presence*, Anne Phillips usefully contrasts these two aspects of representation as the 'politics of presence' versus the 'politics of ideas'. In descriptive representation *who* represents (who is present) is most important, whereas in responsive representation *what* is represented (which ideas) is primary. However, after defining these two types of representation, Phillips argues that divorcing one from the other is counterproductive and perhaps even impossible.[4] Going beyond simplistic dichotomies, it is clear that in descriptive representation the assumption is that the 'ordinary' people so chosen will bring with them a representative sample of the ideas, beliefs and predispositions of the wider populace, while in responsive representation the voters are *very* interested in exactly who (and in particular which leader) will be doing the representing. The two forms of representation are always mixed.

Since the 1960s, however, the argument that descriptive representation is irrelevant to good lawmaking has increasingly come under attack, largely by the feminist and black civil rights movements, and the politics of identity in general. Phillips says:

> In this major reframing of the problems of democratic equality, the separation between 'who' and 'what' is to be represented, and the subordination of the first to the sec-

ond, is very much up for question. The politics of ideas is being challenged by an alternative politics of presence.[5]

Mandatory quotas for women in politics initially appeared in a few Nordic countries in the mid-1970s. It has been emulated by many countries such as post-apartheid South Africa, India (where it is also applied to the disadvantaged lower castes), Brazil, Argentina and Afghanistan, to name just a few. Indeed, Afghanistan had a higher proportion of women in parliament than the UK until the 2015 election – the UK parliament now has 29 per cent women, whereas war-torn Afghanistan has 28 per cent.[6] Outside Scandinavia, a few, typically left-leaning political parties in Europe have internal goals for the percentage of female candidates and elected representatives. But progress has been slow, and the shift fiercely resisted, often by appeals to how quotas may reduce accountability since 'it is hard to conceive of accountability except in terms of policies and programmes and ideas'.[7] The argument for quotas, however, rests firmly on the historical fact of the structural exclusion of women – if we assume that men are not somehow innately suited to politics and predisposed to better lawmaking, then it is clear that they have no right to monopolise legislative assemblies. Descriptive representation can work towards reversing histories of exclusion; its promotion should always be argued for in terms of anticipated policy changes, not only around election times, but perhaps more importantly between them.

Clarissa Rile Hayward states it clearly when she says: 'in a political society that is both internally divided and hierarchical, people who are disadvantaged by structural inequalities should be represented by people who share their positions of disadvantage'.[8] It takes little imagination to appreciate that 'the perspectives of the dominant differ systematically from those of the disadvantaged' and that, even if the representatives are genuinely motivated by the public good, they may not understand how best to pursue it.[9] Furthermore, between elections, politicians:

> ... respond to new conflicts, new crises, new opportunities and possibilities. They develop, evaluate, and debate about new proposals. Political representatives, when they engage in deliberation with one another, engage in debates that cannot be charted or plotted in advance. Hence descriptive representation (one might argue), because it brings to deliberative forums people who share at least some of the

relevant experiences and perspectives of the disadvantaged, is crucial for democratic politics under conditions of structural inequality.[10]

Representative democracy is meant to be about more than raw preferences and opinions. Hayward says: 'Representation promotes legitimacy in government, not by tracking *any* interests, but by tracking people's post-deliberative interests, or the interests as they (would) understand them after subjecting them to free, equal, and public rational argumentation.'[11] If the tracking and aggregating of the interests of constituents were all representatives were required to do, then there would be little need for public debate, where a crucial element of politics involves justifying and convincing people, the media and the political establishment why certain interests should take precedence over others. One hopes that politicians are affected by the consideration of counter-arguments. As Phillips states: 'There is a strong dose of realism here. Representatives *do* have autonomy, which is why it matters who those representatives are.'[12]

Hayward, however, believes that even descriptive representation will not protect groups of disadvantaged people who, unlike women, form numerical minorities – it only 'gives voice to [their] perspectives and [their] claims'.[13] Hayward is dubious that, even if the point of view of a minority is articulated in a legislature, it will lead to changes in policy. Yet there are two sides to this coin. If the numerical minority is the richest 10 or 20 per cent of society who are structurally *privileged*, then reducing their presence in assemblies to only 10 or 20 per cent should have significant consequences.

It is also clear, from the highly personalised nature of modern politics, that it does matter who does the representing. No matter how hard those advocating a 'politics of ideas' argue that representatives somehow track, or follow, the wishes of their constituents – and as such the gender, age or socio-economic status of a representative should not matter – studying any election campaign makes it abundantly obvious that the personal qualities of leaders matter just as much as, and perhaps more than, their policies or ability to track the preferences of their constituents.

Elections are a device for selecting *someone* and not simply an idea. It could be argued that leaders are the personification of a particular political party, and political parties are a convenient shorthand voters use to denote a collection of ideas they identify with. Then again, the vast majority of people have no idea what the detailed policies are of the party they vote for, and if the shorthand is as simple as 'left-wing equals tax-and-spend and right-wing equals cut-and-save', then the historical record of politicians in power convincingly contradicts such a simplistic categorisation.

Nonetheless, as political parties are a key feature of modern democratic representation, one can directly measure the degree of representation in our legislative assemblies by comparing the proportion of votes cast for each party to the proportion of seats each party obtains. If it is postulated that people vote for a person or party that reliably represents their interests, then the degree to which a country's electoral system disproportionately excludes smaller parties from parliaments can be seen as a measure of how unrepresentative the system is. However, it must be clearly stated at the outset that disadvantaging small parties is often a deliberate consequence of electoral system design, argued for in terms of increased governmental stability, or for the (supposed) clear line of accountability between a constituency and a single member of parliament, or as a disincentive to the splintering of parties.

As outlined above, plurality-majority electoral systems, including the first-past-the-post system typical of the US and UK and the alternative vote used for the House of Representatives in Australia, often lead to two dominant parties.[14] The argument against them taps into one of the fundamental criticisms of any majoritarian decision-making process: the need to protect minorities and ensure that their voice is not excluded from the legislative process. Proportional-representation systems are an alternative that leads to many more parties attracting votes and obtaining parliamentary seats.[15]

Figure 4 compares the percentage of the vote to the percentage of seats that the three major parties or coalitions received in recent national elections to the legislative houses of parliament in the UK, Australia, Germany and the Netherlands. The discrepancy between each pair of columns highlights how unrepresentative a system is, where a party received disproportionately more (or fewer) seats than votes. Wherever one falls on the question of plurality-majority versus proportional electoral systems, it is clear that the latter – used, for example, in the Netherlands – is more representative of the people's votes than the former, as used in the UK.

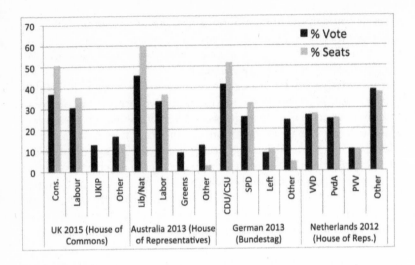

Figure 4: Percentage of votes compared to percentage of legislative seats.

By comparing the third-placed parties in Figure 4 (UKIP in the UK, Greens in Australia, Left in Germany and PVV in the Netherlands), we can see why voters for minor parties in plurality-majority systems should feel discriminated against. The UK is an extreme example. UKIP received a third of the vote of the winning Conservatives, yet this translated into only one seat in parliament. Similarly, the Australian Greens' vote of almost 10 per cent resulted in only a single seat in their so-called House of Representatives – a clear indictment of the unrepresentativeness of the system.

The Netherlands, on the other hand, has one of the purest forms of proportional voting in the world, with all the discrepancies being less than 1 per cent. If a party earns 10 per cent of the votes, they get 10 per cent of the seats in parliament. The German system is a mix of two systems; however, the proportional element is deliberately used to correct the disproportionality of the plurality-majority part. It also incorporates a five-percentage minimum-vote threshold to achieve representation, making it significantly less proportional than the Netherlands for smaller parties. Nevertheless, it still does markedly better than the UK or Australia if your primary concern is that most people's vote should contribute equally to the make-up of parliament. The US only deserves a mention here for two reasons: in the 2012 election, the Democrats actually obtained more votes than the Republicans for the House of Representatives, but gained eight per cent fewer seats; and the two-party system is so stable that the exceptional case of Bernie Sanders's long career as an independent congressman (prior to and after his running as a Democratic presidential candidate in 2016) stands out starkly against the long history of almost complete Democrat and Republican domination of Congress.

Obviously, many more people vote for smaller parties in the proportional systems since they know their vote will not be wasted, and it also seems that 'proportional representation systems tend to be associated with higher turnout'.[16] Plurality-majority systems limit what parties people will vote for, and restrict the diversity of voices present in parliaments, which perhaps contributes to a more adversarial style of politicking.

There are also large swathes of residents in every democratic country who are not represented at all due to the simple fact that they do not, or cannot, vote in elections.

It is overly simplistic to dismiss those who do not vote as lazy, since voter participation has consistently been shown to be systematically biased in favour of older and more privileged citizens.[17] Indeed, before the 2012 US election, an 'assault on voter rights' in several key battleground states (Florida in particular) by Republican-controlled state legislatures occurred. The methods of assault included instituting hurdles to voter registration, and the banning and attempted purging of previously eligible voters. Ostensibly, the new rules were intended to eliminate voter fraud, an almost non-existent problem, and since its general effect was to disenfranchise the less educated and poor, who predominantly vote Democrat, it is easy to be suspicious of the Republicans' motives.[18]

Members of our societies who cannot vote include those obviously unable – infants and the mentally incapacitated – and those less obviously excluded – some prisoners in some places, non-citizen permanent residents and adolescents. It is far from clear that the needs of the groups barred from voting will be necessarily considered and given due prominence in the legislative process, and in most cases there have been various movements to empower them or delegate their votes to others.

The minimum age for voting displays a clear historical trend downwards:

In general, a minimum voting age between 23 and 30 was the rule until later in the 20th century, when it was set at 18. At the beginning of the 20th century, it was 24 in Aus-

THE END OF POLITICIANS

tria, 25 in Belgium, Prussia, the Netherlands and Norway, and 30 in Denmark. In Sweden the voting age for general elections was lowered to 21 from 23 only in 1945. In the UK, where women had been granted the right to vote in 1918, the voting age for women then was 30; it was reduced to 21 in 1928, and the voting age for both men and women was further lowered to 18 in 1969. In France, the right to vote at age 18 was also established in 1969. Most recently, the German state (*Land*) of Lower Saxony (*Niedersachsen*) lowered the voting age in local elections to 16 in 1995. Other German states have since followed, and three Austrian states (*Länder*) have also introduced a voting age of 16 in local elections.[19]

The 26th Amendment to the United States Constitution lowered the voting age to 18 in 1971. In Scotland, the voting age was lowered to 16 in time for the Scottish referendum on independence in 2014.

The idea of giving extra votes to parents with dependent children (sometimes called Demeny voting) has variously been proposed and debated in Germany, Hungary and Japan, often as a counter to the coming demographic domination by the elderly in those countries and its assumed distortion of public policy.[20]

New Zealand, one of the first places to enfranchise women, has again led most of the world by expanding the national franchise to all permanent residents regardless of citizenship. If you pay taxes you should be represented, so the old slogan goes. The European Union (EU) has also extended the franchise to non-national residents from other EU countries for local and European Parliament elections, and several countries extend this right to 'third-country nationals' as well.[21] In 2014, Paris ran a participatory budgeting process that allowed all Paris residents, regardless of age and nationality, to vote.[22]

The usual exclusion of children, adolescents, many immigrants and others means that the actual percentage of the total population who select our representatives is much lower than voter turnout statistics portray. Only around one in five (21 per cent) of the population of the US actually voted for their elected president in 2012. In some states with large immigrant populations, such as California, almost 20 per cent of the adult population are disenfranchised. In EU parliamentary elections, voter turnout has steadily declined to below 50 per cent of eligible voters, so it can also be assumed that those elected to office receive direct endorsement from perhaps 20 per cent of the total population of their constituency.[23] If 80 per cent of residents in an area do not endorse a Member of the European Parliament (MEP), then in what sense is the MEP representative?

Reducing descriptive representation to a study of how closely the composition of parliaments reflects the voting results is, however, very limiting. This simple measure of the unrepresentativeness of representative democracies says nothing at all about the under-representation of women, or the demographic and socio-economic discrepancies between those elected and the general populace. The vehement anti-democracy advocate who would become the second president of the US, John Adams, expressed curious descriptive sympathies when he stated in 1776 that a representative assembly 'should be in miniature an exact portrait of the people at large. It should think, feel, reason, and act like them.'[24] The figures below show the distribution of gender, age, ethnicity and wealth of US politicians, compared to the general populace. The portrait of US society painted by its national congress is, as expected, highly distorted.

Figures 5 and 6 compare the age and gender distribution of the general population of the US to that of the members of the 113th US Congress, resulting from the 2012 elections, which had a record high number of female members.

Figure 5: Distribution of age and gender in the US.

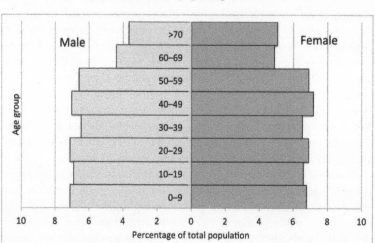

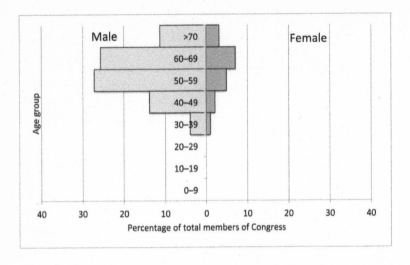

Figure 6: Distribution of age and gender in the US Congress.

As expected, the most striking feature of Figure 6 is the overall bias towards older men. The severe gender imbalance reflects those in other spheres, such as business management, the judiciary, finance, entertainment and the media. In several countries, a majority of people believe the gender imbalance needs to be 'urgently' addressed.[25] Sweden, the Netherlands and Finland have made remarkable progress, using a variety of tools, such as mandated quotas, towards equality of representation both in politics and in corporate boardrooms. In Norway in 2008, women accounted for 43 per cent of the board members of large companies, and the Swedish parliament in 2007 had 47 per cent women. 'There has been a steady, if slow, improvement' towards eroding the gender bias, at least in Europe.[26] The expansion of the franchise to include women may have been a necessary step in this process; however, it has taken several further decades and the emergence of the modern feminist movement for the structural exclusions and overt discrimination and sexism to be slowly exposed and somewhat overturned. There remains much vocal opposition to proactive attempts to further address the gender imbalance; the very vehemence of the opposition probably highlights the strength and broad gains made by feminism. The structural and cultural barriers that bias the electoral system towards men undermine the legitimacy of parliaments. The inadequate incorporation in policy of the concerns of women, who still undertake the vast majority of the (often unpaid) care-related activities in our society, must reduce the substantive quality of legislation. In the UK in 2010, a government Speaker's Conference on Parliamentary Representation report concluded 'that there is a real need to make political parties reflective of the communities they serve. Democracy will be better delivered when people feel that there is a voice representing them within the political process.'[27]

If eradicating the gender bias is increasingly seen as important, why not also the age bias? As noted above, the voting age has been decreasing steadily and seems set to continue to do so, although age restrictions on standing for office are still common. For example, in the US the president must be at least 35 and senators 30 years of age; court challenges to these age restrictions have failed, as standing for office has not been interpreted as a fundamental democratic right. Will this belief that older equals smarter eventually go the way of the once equally common belief that male equals smarter? Most countries require airline pilots to retire at 65, and champion chess masters are often under the age of 30, yet many politicians are over 65 and almost none of them under 30. Is it self-evident that young adults do not possess the requisite abilities to contribute meaningfully to political discussions, and that older adults can be trusted to fully and equally consider the needs and desires of the under-represented age groups? Given that definitions and objective measures of 'intelligence' or 'wisdom' or 'maturity' are notoriously difficult, it is a highly dubious claim that older adults are more intelligent than younger adults. Intelligence is multifaceted and, to highlight but one example, it is postulated that one of our most important abilities, fluid intelligence, peaks in early adulthood, while crystallised intelligence remains stable or perhaps increases until mid–late adulthood.[28] What is beyond doubt is that there is a complex relationship between age and intelligence.

While there appears to be little evidence to justify the exclusion of young adults from positions of power, there is certainly none to justify the bias of representation against ethnic minorities displayed in Figure 7.

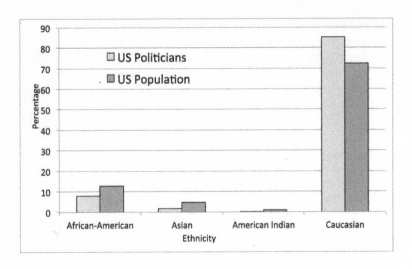

Figure 7: Ethnicity of the US population compared to members of Congress.

A few attempts have been made to correct biases against those in under-represented ethnicities. Phillips details several examples in the US where electoral districts have been redefined ('gerrymandered') to produce overwhelmingly black constituencies to increase the likelihood of the election to office of black politicians, although, more often than not, gerrymandering electoral districts is done to benefit one of the two main parties.[29] New Zealand has several mandated seats in its national parliament for the representation of its indigenous Maori people.

Given all these imbalances, few people would be surprised by perhaps the most shocking bias: the difference in the wealth distribution of US citizens and the national politicians elected to represent them, shown in Figure 8. This figure shows the approximate percentage of people within a given wealth bracket for US families (grey line) and US members of Congress (darker line). The monetary values are on a logarithmic scale, meaning that the units go from $1,000 to $10,000 to $100,000, etc.

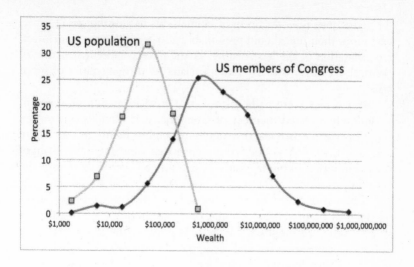

Figure 8: Wealth of US families compared to members of Congress.

While wealth does not follow a normal ('bell curve') distribution throughout society (the top 20 per cent of Americans own approximately 85 per cent of the country's wealth), what Figure 8 shows is the percentage of US families in each range of wealth. The median US family wealth in 2010 was $77,300, and approximately 70 per cent of US families have between $10,000 and $300,000 in equity. In contrast, the wealth of US national politicians has a (lognormal) mean equivalent to $1.16 million – 52.3 per cent of them are millionaires. While certain qualifications for office such as age, residency and citizenship have always existed, being a millionaire is becoming a *de facto* qualification.

This is not an accurate portrait of US society in miniature. If Congress is fast becoming a club for millionaires, then it surely skews and biases the legislation produced so that business as usual prevails over urgent goals such as preventing dangerous climate change. It goes far towards explaining why it is such a struggle to index the minimum wage to inflation, or to implement a wealth tax, or to increase or institute inheritance taxes, or to raise taxes for the highest income bracket. What kind of legislation would be produced if the politicians did represent the US population at large and around 15 per cent of them were receiving food stamps to feed themselves and their families?[30] If gender balance among our representatives is important, is the wealth imbalance less so? As Phillips notes, if one is to argue for guaranteed representation of women due to existing structures of exclusion, then one should presumably also argue for the guaranteed representation of the less wealthy, as 'the most persistent structure of political exclusion is surely that associated with inequalities of social class'.[31]

If a wager were to be placed on the socio-economic status of a randomly selected member of Congress, it is obvious where one should place the bet: on that random member being an old, white and rich man.[32] A politics of presence that fundamentally changes the composition of our legislative assemblies will certainly change the laws they produce.

The existing system, whereby it is assumed our representatives need *not* be a representative sample of the community in the way that, say, a court jury supposedly is, rests heavily on the assumption that politicians are responsive and accountable to the wishes of their constituents. Defenders of this point of view like to proclaim that the people, through the act of voting, are in ultimate control. If politicians do not give voters what they want, they will be kicked out. Or if no party offers a policy programme that a large enough group of people want, then a new party will spring up to fill the gap. There is a strong implied analogy here between politics and market choice: consumers (or voters) simply get what they ask for, and if a market opportunity exists for a new product (or policy programme), a new company (or political party) will soon move to fill and 'profit' from it.

This argument is disingenuous for several reasons. The most obvious, if we continue with the market metaphor, is that existing parties dominate like a business duopoly in a well-developed industry – especially so, as shown above, where electoral design explicitly favours two major parties. Also, national election campaigns cost millions of dollars and consume thousands of hours of paid and volunteer time, so it is exceedingly difficult (though not impossible) for new parties to overcome the prohibitively expensive barriers to entering the (political) marketplace. Dominant parties in many countries were formed even before universal suffrage became the norm, and have maintained their dominance for several decades. Furthermore, companies do not merely fulfil desires – through advertising and branding they also create and artificially stimulate them. Similarly, political parties do not only respond to concerns; they also work hard to define and constrain the political agenda.

Party members, where they control the pre-selection of candidates, also wield inordinate power. Especially in a two-party system, if candidate selection is controlled by highly ideological party activists, then the loyalty and accountability of those elected will necessarily be distorted by the need to appease local party members. King notes that in the UK:

> Voters cannot vote for whomever they like. In practice, they can vote only for one of however many candidates the parties in their locality choose to nominate. Especially in safe seats – in recent years some 80 per cent of the total – that means that the dominant local party, in effect, decides all by itself who the local MP is going to be.[33]

King goes on to lament that members' 'power has waxed as their numbers have waned. Sometimes they resemble a small tail wagging a big dog.'[34] Even if ultimately people get to vote, the choice is far less significant if the options are so tightly constrained by party members.

The claim that elections give people meaningful choice (or respond to what they want) has been most damningly undermined by the 2016 US election and the preceding presidential primaries. Although it is certainly an extreme case, opinion polls consistently showed that more than 50 per cent of people viewed Hillary Clinton unfavourably and around 60 per cent disliked Donald Trump – they were 'among the worst-rated presidential candidates of the last seven decades'.[35] When the choice for president is about who you dislike the least, there would appear to be something seriously wrong with the most powerful democracy on the planet and with the idea that elections are in any direct way responsive to the wishes of the people.

Elections are notoriously blunt instruments to act as the core mechanism of accountability in modern democracies. In *Democracy for Realists: Why Elections Do Not Produce Responsive Government*, Christopher Achen and Larry Bartels, both of Princeton University, systematically and thoroughly undermine this exceedingly common 'folk theory of democracy'. They detail how the 'conventional thinking about democracy has collapsed in the face of modern social-scientific research… The populist ideal of electoral democracy, for all its elegance and attractiveness, is largely irrelevant in practice, leaving elected officials mostly free to pursue their own notions of the public good or to respond to party and interest group preferences.'[36] Their overwhelming evidence is of voter choice being determined by habitual, socially determined behaviour. Voters 'typically make choices not on the basis of policy preferences or ideology, but on the basis of who they are – their social identities'.[37] They also undermine the notion of retrospective voting, whereby voters theoretically reward or punish those in government, by showing how inconsistent and incoherent such acts often are – it is 'group and partisan loyalties' that determine the behaviour of most voters.[38]

If electoral choice is so often tightly constrained, and most people vote to reaffirm their group identity, then are governments tracking anyone's interests? The answer probably will not come as a surprise.

Bartels's *Unequal Democracy* and Martin Gilens's *Affluence and Influence* undermine the assumption that politicians reliably track their constituents' opinions.[39] Bartels uncovers a clear correlation between US politicians' votes in Congress and middle- and especially upper-class interests, on both sides of the political spectrum. Gilens's research shows the same pattern of correlation between public opinion and implemented policies. If politicians in the US are tracking anyone's interests, the statistical evidence demonstrates that it is overwhelmingly the interests of the wealthy.

Bartels's work explores the 'glaring disjunctions between the predictions of simple majoritarian models and actual patterns of policy making in the United States over the past half-century'.[40] If politicians did simply respond to their constituents' wishes, then why have 'senators representing exactly the same constituents frequently exhibited markedly different ideological behaviour'?[41] Party politics is very persuasive: many politicians will vote according to the wishes of the executive or cabinet. The Washington model, which supposedly has *more* freedom from party constraints, is often contrasted to the Westminster model, where ideology is made explicit through the use of political officials called 'whips', who attempt to ensure representatives toe the party line. Bartels's analyses of politicians' behaviour in the US 'underscore the immense significance of elite ideology in the making of American public policy', which has 'much more to do with partisan politics and ideology than with public sentiment'.[42]

Bartels further highlights the 'profound difficulties faced by ordinary citizens in connecting specific policy proposals to their own values and interests'.[43] For example, a majority of people who professed to believe the wealthy should pay more taxes were against a specific inheritance tax proposal that would have, in its application, only affected the rich. Those with vested (ideological or financial) interests will always try to actively spin their opinion to derail policy or score political points. Successful politicians make careers out of dissembling.

Even more damning, however, is the analysis by Bartels showing that elites listen predominately to their own:

> I find that senators in this period were vastly more responsive to affluent constituents than to constituents of modest means. Indeed, my analyses indicate that the views of constituents in the upper third of the income distribution received about 50 per cent more weight than those in the middle third, with even larger disparities on specific salient roll call votes. Meanwhile, the views of constituents in the bottom third of the income distribution received no weight at all in the voting decisions of their senators. Far from being 'considered as political equals,' they were entirely unconsidered in the policy-making process.[44]

In *Affluence and Influence*, Gilens finds a similar correlation between expressed preferences and policy outcomes:

> Few will be surprised that the link between preferences and policies turns out to be stronger for higher-income Americans than for the poor. But the magnitude of this difference, and the inequality in representation that I find even between the affluent and the slightly less well-off, suggest that the political system is tilted very strongly in favor of those at the top of the income distribution... The complete lack of government responsiveness to the poor is disturbing and seems consistent only with the most cynical views of American politics. These results indicate that when preferences between the well-off and the poor diverge, government policy bears absolutely no relationship to the degree of support or opposition among the poor.[45]

Gilens goes on to test if this is because middle-income and upper-income preferences are similar, and, thus, in a majoritarian system, the disregard for the poor could actually indicate a well-functioning, responsive democracy. He finds:

> ... that median-income Americans fare no better than the poor when their policy preferences diverge from those of the well-off... [G]overnment policy appears to be fairly

responsive to the well-off and virtually unrelated to the desires of low- and middle-income citizens.[46]

Of course, the low- and middle-income citizens do get what they want sometimes: in those instances when their preferences are aligned with the preferences of the rich.[47]

If politicians do respond to their constituents, then they over-whelmingly respond to the richer ones. Possibly these affluent constituents are simply part of a politician's social milieu. It is the group of people from which the politicians themselves are drawn; we should not be surprised that politicians' votes display a strong correlation with the interests of their own socio-economic class. According to King, the 'well-off' in the UK:

> ... have interests in common. They know it. They typically, though not invariably, have common values and a similar outlook on life. They see a good deal of each other. They are disposed to look after one another. Their children go to the same or similar schools. They drive, or are driven, in similar cars. Even if they never meet, they recognize each other at a distance. The well-off are clearly, by a wide margin, the dominant interest in Britain today, even though there is no formal organization that unites them and uniquely represents their interests.[48]

In attempting to explain the bias in the US, Bartels rules out the well-documented fact that many forms of political participation (voting, contacting an elected member, signing petitions) show a bias towards wealthier citizens. Although inconclusive, the one factor that appears relevant is the influence of political donations, which come predominately from the more affluent.[49] In any case, whatever the *reason* for this representational inequality, it is the *fact* of its existence that is most disturbing.

This evidence suggests it is naïve to argue that the people are in any direct or meaningful way in control of politicians as they go about their legislative business. Since politicians of all stripes are, in general, far more responsive to the wealthy, arguing that voting selects candidates most responsive to their constituents is easily dismissed as overly simplistic, especially in a strongly partisan political system.

Given the reality of limited direct control, some may invest their hopes in the stubbornly popular myth that the process of election somehow ensures that those elected will act as guardians of the common good.[50] However, this has been so thoroughly derided by the rational-choice theorists (see Chapter Three), and undermined by our competitive hyper-individualistic society as to be hard to believe.[51] As also noted above, it is ironic that the fight to defend liberal capitalism against communism by propounding narrow self-interest as the most important motivator can be held somewhat responsible for undermining any faith in the benevolent guardianship of our elected representatives. The countries that today continue to promote these ideals of guardianship are mostly authoritarian regimes, with Iran (and its Guardian Council), China and North Korea leading the pack in their hubristic claim that government exists solely to serve the people. It appears, in China at least, that in the process of 'serving the people' the top officials are becoming even wealthier than US politicians: a Bloomberg report found that the wealth of the National People's Congress's 70 richest members totalled US$90 billion – they added more to their wealth in one year than the combined net worth of the entire US Congress.[52]

Honest observers today agree and openly admit that what occurs in our democracies is a very broadly constrained bargaining among elites. Dahl puts representative democracy's 'dark side' thus:

> Most citizens in democratic countries are aware of it; for the most part they accept it as a part of the price of representation.
>
> The dark side is this: under a representative government, citizens often delegate enormous discretionary authority over decisions of extraordinary importance. They delegate authority not only to their elected representatives but, by an even more indirect and circuitous route, they delegate authority to administrators, bureaucrats, civil servants, judges, and at a still further remove to international organizations. Attached to the institutions of polyarchal democracy that help citizens to exercise influence over the conduct and decisions of their government is a nondemocratic process, bargaining among political and bureaucratic elites.
>
> In principle, elite bargaining takes place within limits set through democratic institutions and processes. But these limits are often broad, popular participation and con-

trol are not always robust, and the political and bureaucratic elites possess great discretion.[53]

Gilens concludes that the 'patterns of responsiveness' he uncovers
'often correspond more closely to a plutocracy than a democracy'.[54]
Bartels admits:

> ... our political system seems to function not as a 'democ-
> racy' but as an 'oligarchy.' If we insist on flattering our-
> selves by referring to it as a democracy, we should be clear
> that it is a starkly unequal democracy... Whatever elec-
> tions may be doing, they are not forcing elected officials to
> cater to the policy preferences of the 'median voter.'[55]

John Ferejohn and Frances Rosenbluth, in their chapter in *Political
Representation* entitled 'Electoral Representation and the Aristocratic
Thesis', concur:

> ... the actions of political agents are very hard to observe,
> and elections, the typical way of disciplining political
> agents, are a crude and imperfect way to reward officials...
> [As such] elected representatives usually have a great deal
> of latitude to pursue their goals... [P]olicies are likely to
> be chosen that will please those who have effective control
> over access to office such as contributors and [party]
> activists.[56]

Indeed, it is part of the thesis presented above that this is why our
so-called representative democracy triumphed: because it is an unrepresentative system that, with the active consent of most people, delivers a very loosely constrained rule into the hands of the powerful
and wealthy. Reflecting on the history of this triumph, Dunn notes:
'Madison's early-nineteenth-century discovery that universal male
suffrage was no real threat to property was made independently, if
appreciably later, in well over half the countries of Europe, not always
by direct experience, but by even more obvious inference.'[57] Extending the franchise to those without property did not change the composition of parliaments, just as extending it to women did not change
the composition substantially until the arrival of quotas and modern
feminism several decades later. It will take a passionate and sustained
social change movement to alter the status quo.

If bargaining among elites is what we have, and the rewards of fame and power for those who win are so tempting, it is no surprise that Machiavellian means are often employed.

Nepotism, cronyism, privilege and corruption have surely always been components of every system of power. 'In the early nineteenth century… governments such as the British had shared out the correctly named "offices of profit under the *Crown*" and lucrative sinecures amongst their kinsmen and dependents', says Hobsbawm.[58] As pointed out above, in the US in the 19th and early 20th centuries a change of government meant a wholesale exchange of bureaucrats as the victors handed out jobs to supporters and financial backers, who were then expected to 'donate' part of their wages back to the victorious party.

After the extension of the franchise to a large percentage of male adults, but before the widespread use of the 'Australian (secret) ballot', open voting by a show of hands 'was carried out in public by means of threats, nods and winks… Plying [the voters] with grog and grub was also a favourite device.'[59] If you did not vote according to the wishes of your landlord or employer, who had just given you free food and drink, you were taking obvious risks.

Even now, it is commonplace for large party donors and effective fundraisers to get posts as ambassadors: in 2013, the average 'price' for a valuable ambassadorship under President Obama was US$1.8 million.[60] Although the scandal of 'cash for peerages' to the House of Lords in 2006–7 (where several men nominated for peerages were found to have made large, undisclosed loans to the Labour Party) did not result in criminal convictions, that may have only been because those involved were not foolish enough to enter into explicit agreements.

Ever since the invention of radio, and then television, the broadcast media has played a key role in politics. Radio and television:

> … magnified the political function of the mass media, which now reached into every household, providing by far the most powerful means of communication from the public sphere to the private men, women and children. Their capacity to discover and publish what authority wished to keep quiet, and to give expression to public feelings which were not, or could no longer be, articulated by the formal

mechanisms of democracy, made them into major actors on the public scene. Politicians used them and were frightened of them... [I]t became evident that the media were a far more important component of the political process than parties and electoral systems.[61]

Media tycoons often explicitly back certain candidates (in Italy, Silvio Berlusconi actually *became* a candidate), and this must have an effect on the content issuing from their media outlets. The importance of this cannot be overstated. As Manuel Castells notes: 'politics becomes increasingly played out in the space of the media. Leadership is personalized, and image-making is power-making... [W]hoever the political actors and whatever their orientations, they exist in the power game through and by the media.'[62]

Since 'personalities are considered at least as important as political parties', individual politicians build up extensive networks of contacts within media establishments.[63] As there is far less identification between voters and a particular party, the personality of the leader as portrayed in the media is increasingly important, and parties 'tend to become instruments in the service of a leader'.[64]

The continued importance of the media could not be more adequately demonstrated than by the network of corruption and dubious connections exposed by the police investigations surrounding the News International phone-hacking scandal in the UK, and the resulting criminal charges, convictions and Leveson Inquiry of 2011–12. The trail of money and influence among politics, the media and the police that came to light left even the most cynical of observers flabbergasted.

Andy Coulson, editor of the *News of the World* (part of the News International empire) resigned when the offences first came to light, but went on to become the director of communications for the UK's then prime minister, David Cameron. When the scandal hit the headlines again a few years later, he was charged, convicted and imprisoned. Cameron admitted that 'we all did too much cosying up to Rupert Murdoch', but claimed that this was a continuation of normal governmental behaviour.[65] He was undoubtedly correct: former UK prime minister Tony Blair is reported to be the godfather of Rupert Murdoch's daughter, Grace.[66]

Maintaining favourable relationships with the media certainly benefits both political parties and the media under normal circumstances. Other industries must work harder to influence policy. The

British financial services industry, for example, employed 800 people and spent US$142 million over a 12-month period neutering or killing off unfavourable government plans after the 2008 economic crisis, according to a Bureau of Investigative Journalism report.[67] OpenSecrets.org documents the 12,000 active US lobbyists and their annual US$3.3 billion in spending – which is more than 20 lobbyists, spending on average at least 6 million dollars each, for every member of the US Congress. In Brussels, it is estimated that 15,000 lobbyists buzz around EU institutions and their staff.[68]

Many corporations are in turn actively pursued by politicians as potential donors to political parties that need many millions of dollars to run election campaigns. The UK Conservative party secretary was recorded by undercover journalists offering potential donors 'awesome' and 'premier league' access to leading government figures for donations over a quarter of a million pounds. US candidates seem to spend at least as much time chasing donors as they do chasing votes. And since the US Supreme Court sanctioned Super PACs (Public Action Committees) in 2010, these organisations can avoid the legislated limits imposed on direct donations to congressional campaigns by claiming to be independent of, and not coordinating directly with, a candidate or political party. They can now raise and spend unlimited funds on political campaigns during election time. The amounts spent in each US federal election is reportedly even more than that spent by lobbying organisations annually, rising to the obscene level of US$6.3 billion for the 2012 election, of which Barack Obama and Mitt Romney (the Democrat and Republican candidates, respectively) approached US$1 billion each for their individual campaigns.[69]

The list of corrupting and corrupt practices appears endless: the quashing by a British prime minister of an investigation into bribery in the Al-Yamamah arms deal with the Saudis; charities set up as fronts for networking defence personnel and their lobbyists (Atlantic Bridge); repeated revelations of corporate donors receiving government contracts (or peerages to the House of Lords in the UK); and expenses scandals returning with sickening regularity, to name but a few.[70] In India, around a quarter of the national members of parliament were facing criminal trials in the 2000s, and in Brazil the Supreme Court banned corporate donations to candidates and parties after a series of high-profile corruption scandals.[71] George Monbiot calls our democracy a 'dictatorship of vested interests' and documents many more examples and areas of corporate influence in his book *Captive State*.[72] Al Gore would appear to agree with Monbiot: 'Amer-

ican democracy has been hacked... The US Congress... is now inca-
pable of passing laws without permission from the corporate lobbies
and other special interests that control campaign finances.'[73] Who
pays the piper, calls the tune, it is said. In Britain, even David
Cameron claimed: 'The far too cosy relationship between politics,
government, business and money has tainted our politics for too
long.'[74] Admittedly, he was in opposition at the time and trying to
score political points.

Unsurprisingly, anti-corruption and populist (anti-elite) movements have proved popular in such an environment. The Five Star
Movement in Italy gained around 25 per cent of the vote in the
2013 national elections by calling for existing MPs to 'Pack your
bags!'. Claudia Chwalisz, in *The Populist Signal*, postulates that the
recent surge in support for parties such as UKIP in the UK is a direct
response to anti-elite sentiment and widespread feelings of political
disenfranchisement.[75] The 2016 'Brexit' vote for Britain to leave the
EU has been interpreted by many in a similar light. In India, anti-corruption movements and hunger strikes by social activist Anna Hazare
in the last two decades have led to the Common Man Party winning
40 per cent of the seats in the 2013 Delhi state assembly election. The
rise of such groups has many established parties rattled.

Politics has been captured by corporations, the media, the powerful and the wealthy. Or, rather, it has remained captured, for the
claim that it is now captured implies that there was a previous time
when it was not, and even the most cursory glance at the history of
democracy shows that there never was such a time. The profound
shift (in the West at least) of the last 200 years from aristocratic rule
to the hesitant appearance and consolidation of representative democracy dismantled hereditary privileges and replaced them with the
privilege of wealth. We might not be living in a so-called democracy
if this was not so.

It is no wonder that 'politician' regularly ranks as one of the least
respected professions in our society.

Notes

1. Philip Pettit, 'Varieties of Public Representation', in Shapiro *et al.* (eds),
Representation, 66.

2. Pettit, 'Varieties', in Shapiro *et al.* (eds), *Representation*, 69.

3. Pettit, 'Varieties', in Shapiro *et al.* (eds), *Representation*, 71.

4. Phillips, *Presence*, 24–5.

5. Phillips, *Presence*, 5.

6. http://data.worldbank.org/indicator/SG.GEN.PARL.ZS.

7. Phillips, *Presence*, 23. Also Chapter Four and 31, 62, 40, 175.

8. Hayward, 'Making Interest', in Shapiro *et al.* (eds), *Representation*, 114.

9. Hayward, 'Making Interest', in Shapiro *et al.* (eds), *Representation*, 117.

10. Hayward, 'Making Interest', in Shapiro *et al.* (eds), *Representation*, 118.

11. Hayward, 'Making Interest', in Shapiro *et al.* (eds), *Representation*, 120.

12. Phillips, *Presence*, 78.

13. Hayward, 'Making Interest', Shapiro *et al.* (eds), *Representation*, 119–20.

14. Even if King in *Who Governs Britain?* details 'the collapse of the classic two-party system' in the UK (93). His 'collapse' is the increase to approximately one-third of voters who do not vote for either of the two main parties. However, these votes translate into only around 15 per cent of the seats in parliament (see figure 4).

15. See Dahl, *Democracy*, Appendix A, for more details and other references. There are also semi-proportional systems, and within these main groupings of electoral systems the number of differing permutations is impressive.

16. International Institute for Democracy and Electoral Assistance (International IDEA), *Voter Turnout in Western Europe* (IIDEA, 2004), 8. See also Rafael López Pintor and Maria Gratschew, *Voter Turnout Since 1945: A Global Report* (IIDEA, 2002).

17. Arend Lijphart, 'Unequal Participation: Democracy's Unresolved Dilemma', *American Political Science Review*, 1997, Vol. 91, No. 1, 1–14; and Jan E. Leighley and Jonathan Nagler, 'Socioeconomic Class Bias in Turnout, 1964–1988: The Voters Remain the Same', *American Political Science Review*, 1992, Vol. 86, No. 3, 725–36: 'voters are of higher socioeconomic status than nonvoters'. IIDEA, *Voter Turnout in Western Europe*, 19: 'the level of education and average income... is associated with increased electoral participation'.

18. See, for example, http://www.nytimes.com/interactive/2014/11/04/us/politics/2014-exit-polls.html?_r=1#us/2014 'Education', 'Income' and 'Race'. Ed Pilkington, 'Key US States Launch Fresh Assault on Voting Rights', *Guardian Weekly*, 3 August 2012.

19. IIDEA, *Voter Turnout in Western Europe*, 15.

20. And not to mention even more radical proposals, such as representatives to speak on behalf of future generations, or on behalf of our natural assets, famously proposed by Christopher Stone in *Should Trees Have Standing?* (Originally published by University of Minnesota, 1972, revised edition by Oxford University Press, 1996).

21. Council Directive 94/80/EC for the municipal elections and Council Directive 93/109/EC for elections to the European Parliament – for example, http://circa.europa.eu/irc/opoce/fact_sheets/info/data/citizen/eligibility/article_7176_en.htm.

22. Richelle Harrison Plesse, 'Paris Gets to Vote on its Pet Projects', *Guardian Weekly*, 17 October 2014.

23. Although these are potentially disingenuous statistics, it makes the point quite sharply. Out of an estimated population of 314 million in the US in 2012, 215 million were eligible to vote (about 68 per cent of the population), of which only 153 million reported to be registered to vote and 129 (133 reported) million actually voted in the presidential election. Of these, 65.9 million voted for the president (21 per cent of the population). Data from http://www.fec.gov/pubrec/fe2012/2012presgeresults.pdf and http://www.census.gov/data/tables/2012/demo/voting-and-registration/p20-568.html. For the EU we assume a turnout of 50 per cent of the approximately 70 per cent of people of voting age, divided by, say, two to three primary candidates.

24. http://www.constitution.org/jadams/thoughts.htm.

25. Of those Europeans polled, 55 per cent thought that the gender ratio in parliament should be addressed 'urgently': Gender Equality in the EU in 2009, http://ec.europa.eu/public_opinion/archives/ebs/ebs_326_en.pdf; 31 per cent of the EU parliament are women, 24 per cent of national parliaments and 11 per cent of the boards of the largest listed EU companies: *Women in European Politics – Time for Action* (2009), http://ec.europa.eu/social/BlobServlet?docId=2052&langId=en); of the top 250 grossing films in the US domestic market in 2011 only 5 per cent were directed by women: http://womenintvfilm.sdsu.edu/files/2011_Celluloid_Ceiling_Exec_Summ.pdf; Sex and Power: Who Runs Britain?, http://fawcettsociety.org.uk/wp-content/uploads/2013/02/Sex-and-Power-2013-FINAL-REPORT.pdf.

26. *Women and Men in Decision-making 2007: Analysis of the Situation and Trends* (2008), http://ec.europa.eu/social/BlobServlet?docId=2034&langId=en; and http://www.ipu.org/wmn-e/world.htm.

27. http://www.parliament.uk/documents/commons-committees/speakers-conference/7824.pdf.

28. Lazar Stankov, 'Aging, Attention, and Intelligence', in *Psychology and Aging*, 1988, Vol. 3, No. 1, 59–74; and Alan S. Kaufman, *IQ Testing 101* (Springer, 2009).

29. Phillips, *Presence*, Chapter Four: 'Race-conscious Districting in the USA'.

30. http://www.cnsnews.com/news/article/ali-meyer/food-stamp-beneficiaries-exceed-46000000-38-straight-months

31. Phillips, *Presence*, 171.

32. And we could continue. We could look at the prior occupations of our representatives (they are disproportionately lawyers) or at the genetic pool from which they are selected (in the UK, even this is startlingly narrow), http://www.theguardian.com/commentisfree/2010/jan/11/commons-mp-expenses-equality-women; and the Speaker's Conference on Parliamentary Representation recommendations: http://www.parliament.uk/documents/commons-committees/speakers-conference/7824.pdf.

33. King, *Britain*, 48; see also 170, 277, 289.

34. King, *Britain*, 58.

35. http://www.theguardian.com/us-news/2016/may/04/donald-trump-hillary-clinton-general-election-analysis; and http://www.gallup.com/poll/193376/trump-leads-clinton-historically-bad-image-ratings.aspx.

36. Achen and Bartels, *Democracy for Realists*, 12, 14.

37. Achen and Bartels, *Democracy for Realists*, 3, 11.

38. Achen and Bartels, *Democracy for Realists*, 18.

39. Larry M. Bartels, *Unequal Democracy: The Political Economy of the New Gilded Age* (Princeton University Press, 2010), 5; Martin Gilens, *Affluence and Influence: Economic Inequality and Political Power in America* (Princeton University Press, 2014).

40. Bartels, *Unequal*, 27.

41. Bartels, *Unequal*, 256.

42. Bartels, *Unequal*, 257, 245.

43. Bartels, *Unequal*, 27; see also 161: 'it [is] equally important to bear in mind the extent to which many ordinary citizens fail to translate their broad values and ideological impulses into consistent views about specific policy issues'.

44. Bartels, *Unequal*, 253–4.

45. Gilens, *Affluence*, 70.

46. Gilens, *Affluence*, 81.

47. Gilens, *Affluence*, 83.

48. King, *Britain*, 140, but see 82–7, where he claims that politicians 'are exceedingly sensitive to the state of public opinion'.

49. Bartels, *Unequal*, 252, 279–82.

50. Dahl, *Democracy*, 74, for a list of arguments against guardianship: 'An advocate of Guardianship confronts a host of formidable practical problems...'

51. Hobsbawm, *Extremes*, 305–6, 334–8: 'The cultural revolution of the late twentieth century can thus best be understood as the triumph of the individual over society.'

52. http://www.bloomberg.com/news/articles/2012-02-26/china-s-billionaire-lawmakers-make-u-s-peers-look-like-paupers; and 'China's Princelings Storing Riches in Caribbean Haven', *Guardian Weekly*, 31 January 2014; see also articles in 30 March 2012 and 2 November 2012 editions.

53. Dahl, *Democracy*, 113; see also 117 and 178.

54. Gilens, *Affluence*, 234.

55. Bartels, *Unequal*, 287.

56. John Ferejohn and Frances Rosenbluth, 'Electoral Representation and the Aristocratic Thesis', in Shapiro *et al.* (eds), *Representation*, 273–4. And more on 281: 'the distinctive slack in political agency is what makes room for the aristocratic hypothesis'.

57. Dunn, *Democracy*, 154.

58. Hobsbawm, *Empire*, 96.

59. Keane, *Democracy*, 527.

60. 'Embassy Posts go to Obama's Big Donors', *Guardian Weekly*, 19 July 2013.

61. Hobsbawm, *Extremes*, 581.

62. Manuel Castells, *The Information Age: Economy, Society and Culture, Volume 1: The Rise of the Network Society*, second edition (Blackwell, 2000), 507.

63. IIDEA, *Voter Turnout in Western Europe*, 19.

64. Manin, *Principles*, 219. See also 220, 232 on his theory that the rise in importance of media skills signifies a change in the type of elite that can win office.

65. http://www.telegraph.co.uk/news/uknews/leveson-inquiry/9227491/David-Camerons-five-secret-meetings-with-Rupert-Murdoch.html.

66. http://www.telegraph.co.uk/news/politics/tony-blair/8740530/Tony-Blair-is-godfather-to-Rupert-Murdochs-daughter.html; King, *Britain*, Chapter Eight.

67. http://www.thebureauinvestigates.com/2012/07/09/revealed-the-93m-city-lobby-machine/.

68. http://corporateeurope.org/lobbycracy.

69. http://www.opensecrets.org/bigpicture/index.php; claim made by Politico website reported in *Guardian Weekly*, 26 October 2012.

70. The Serious Fraud Office closed a corruption investigation into a series of arms deals citing "national and international security" and the "public interest" as reasons (https://www.theyworkforyou.com/lords/?id=2006-12-14d.1711.2). The Atlantic Bridge scandal resulted from Liam Fox's use of a registered charity to pursue political activities, which is illegal. See: https://www.theguardian.com/politics/2011/oct/15/liam-fox-atlantic-bridge.

71. Keane, *Democracy*, 636; 'Poll Donations Ban in Brazil', *Guardian Weekly*, 25 September 2015.

72. George Monbiot, 'The Rich Worlds Veto', http://www.monbiot.com/2002/10/15/the-rich-worlds-veto/.

73. Al Gore, 'The Future: Six Drivers of Global Change', quoted in the *Guardian Weekly*, 15 March 2013.

74. David Cameron, quoted in the *Guardian Weekly*, 26 July 2013. For a list of other scandals see *Guardian Weekly*: 'Peers and MP Caught up in Lobbying Allegations Scandal' (7 June 2013); 'Revolving Door is Revealed as Military Officers Join Arms Firms' (19 October 2012); 'US "Dark Money" Funds Climate Sceptics' (22 February 2013), which details conservative billionaires funding climate denial by funnelling funds through the Donors Trust; 'Party Donors Dominate as New Peers Announced' (9 August 2013). Silvio Berlusconi, ex-prime minister of Italy, has faced 33 trials and was sentenced to four years in jail, but it is unlikely he will ever see the inside of a prison cell.

75. Claudia Chwalisz, *The Populist Signal: Why Politics and Democracy Need to Change* (Rowman & Littlefield International, 2015).

Chapter 5: An Impossible Ideal?

Democracy is an impossible ideal – the way gods would govern themselves, according to Jean-Jacques Rousseau.[1] And gods we most certainly are not. Yet the dream of political equality persists, despite the difficulty of achieving it in such an economically unequal world.

Unattainable ideals can be worth striving for. There are many – a zero road-death toll, or a world without violence – which, while recognising their unattainable nature, we nonetheless try to advance towards.

'In practice democracy has always fallen far short of its ideals,' says Dahl.[2] What is called democracy today, in all its various incarnations, represents some crude historical outcome of the attempt to grapple with the question of how to rule with some degree of legitimacy. It is a constantly disputed compromise between power and the people, and although many would argue for an ideal of informed, disinterested people deliberating in a rational, moral and respectful way, many others would dismiss this as a utopian impossibility.

Yet our current version of democracy 'cannot be all for which we can reasonably hope', as Dunn laments. Surely, as Keane states: 'The history of democracy is still being made', and, in Dahl's words, it is an 'unfinished journey'.[3] Hobsbawm sounds a warning: 'One thing is plain. If humanity is to have a recognizable future, it cannot be by prolonging the past or the present. If we try to build the third millennium on that basis, we shall fail. And the price of failure, that is to say, the alternative to a changed society, is darkness.'[4]

So how can we narrow the gap between ideal and practice? How can we progress democracy's cause? In which direction does technological and social-demographic change seem to be pointing?

The proposals are multitudinous: place quotas around certain demographic groups in parliaments; limit election funding or make parties publicly funded; introduce measures in accounting (at least in the public sector and international institutions) that acknowledge environmental, social and cultural impacts; change to more proportional electoral systems; and lower the voting age or give parents the responsibility for voting on behalf of their children. Other proposals focus on the use of carrots and sticks to make elected representatives more responsive or accountable: institute paid citizens' assemblies to monitor politicians; increase the scrutiny and transparency of decision-making and financial affairs; improve inner-party democracy; and make primary elections compulsory.[5] All of these reforms are based on the assumption that the current system of electoral democracy can be saved; they do not address the fundamental nature of the elite and biased status of our representatives.

In Part Three, it will be argued that sortition can address many of the problems outlined above. It is not a panacea, but it would be an enormous improvement. A randomly selected legislature could be descriptively representative of the adult population. Without elections, there would be no need to chase party donors or pander to the media. And such a legislature would increase the legitimacy of parliaments by bringing an equality and diversity of voices to policy debates that is sorely lacking.

What about international issues? In this era of globalised problems, there are some, like George Monbiot in *The Age of Consent: A Manifesto for a New World Order*, who propose more electoral democracy and a global parliament. The European Parliament represents a very limited step towards this supra-national parliamentary ideal. However, voter turnout for the EU elections is low and the level of interest and support from the general populace continually wanes, as demonstrated starkly by the UK's choice of Brexit in the 2016 referendum. It also suffers from broad democratic deficits in that the elected parliament cannot initiate legislation – most proposals must come from the unelected European Commission. The debate over why voter turnout is waning and disaffection with the EU is on the increase continues, although it does not bode well for an elected global parliament.

Hardt and Negri, and Robert Paehlke, point out that on a global level, governance is already happening.[6] It is a network form of governance, comprising large international institutions (for example, the World Trade Organization, International Monetary Fund, World Bank and United Nations), multinational corporations and large nation states. Between them, a web of standards and institutional practices and norms exists that constitutes a contested field of overlapping jurisdictions, rules and regulations. This is clearly institutionalised bargaining among political, bureaucratic and corporate elites at the global level.

Until recently, there was little hope for change. The current system emerged from the 19th-century struggles against inherited privilege and strict social hierarchy, and firmly established itself in the last half of the 20th century. It influenced, and was influenced by, the cultural and technological transformations of its times: first, the spread of railways and the telegraph, and the emancipation of serfs and peasants and rise of the city and factory; then radio and television and the arrival of a mass consumer culture; and finally the mushrooming of the service and financial sectors of the developed world's economies that accompanied the information-technology revolution.

Society continues to change, perhaps even more rapidly than before. Something profound is happening. The Age of the Spectacle – with its strict divisions between performer and audience, producer and consumer, politician and voter – is coming to an end. The traditional one-to-many transfer of information, typical of television, radio and the hierarchical command structures of business, is being superseded by many-to-many and peer-to-peer exchange between autonomous nodes in a network. Social media is challenging mainstream media, the digital (and real-life) sharing economy is transforming individual ownership, and collaborative creation is pushing aside passive consumption. Participation is becoming the new norm. The information technology that first rose to prominence in the 1970s now permeates nearly every facet of modern existence; new businesses and business models are sprouting and the media landscape is experiencing an earthquake as the new age – the Network Age – is born. It is an age of collaboration, of participation, of openness and transparency. How goods are produced, how profit is extracted, how ideas and culture are dispersed, and how we work, live, play and socialise are all changing rapidly. Part Two focuses on this revolution, before exploring what it may mean for a real democracy better suited to life in the 21st century.

Notes

1. Jean-Jacques Rousseau, *On the Social Contract*: 'Were there a people of Gods, their government would be democratic. So perfect a government is not for men.' See, for example, http://www.bartleby.com/168/304.html.

2. Dahl, *Democracy*, 60.

3. Keane, *Democracy*, xxii; Dahl, *Democracy*, Chapter Fifteen, and 99.

4. Hobsbawm, *Extremes*, 585.

5. Keane, *Democracy*, 823.

6. Michael Hardt and Antonio Negri, *Empire* (Harvard University Press, 2000); Robert C. Paehlke, *Democracy's Dilemma: Environment, Social Equity, and the Global Economy* (The MIT Press, 2004).

Part II: The Network Society

'When we change the way we communicate, we change society.'

–Clay Shirky, *Here Comes Everybody*

'The conceptual models underpinning the participative web (i.e. horizontal vs. vertical; iterative vs. sequential; open vs. proprietary; multiple vs. binary) may be more powerful, and of wider application, than the tools themselves.'

–*Focus on Citizens: Public Engagement for Better Policy and Services*, OECD Studies on Public Engagement

Chapter 6: Talking 'bout a Revolution

The information and communications revolution taking place today surely represents one of the most significant technological, economic and cultural shifts of our time. Networked, participatory and peer-to-peer structures and processes have spread from science and academia to education, finance, the media, manufacturing and society at large. Some of the biggest organisations today owe their wealth or existence to these structures and processes: Amazon, Facebook, Twitter, Wikipedia, eBay, Airbnb and Uber are just a few of the better known. The Internet itself is both an example and an enabler of these networks and networked processes that have become the dominant ideal in many spheres of modern life.

Politics has not been spared these profound changes.

Barack Obama's presidential campaigns learned much from Howard Dean's unsuccessful bid in 2004, when Dean's funds came primarily from small, online donors. In 2008, Obama produced what was at the time probably the most grass-roots campaign in US presidential history, utilising barackobama.com, his website run by Chris Hughes, one of the three co-founders of Facebook. Obama's social networking strategy has changed how US presidential campaigns are conducted.

Civil society has also been transformed as new groups, such as MoveOn.org in the US, 38 Degrees in the UK and GetUp! in Australia, exploit the power of networks. MoveOn was, unsurprisingly, founded by two tech entrepreneurs. With very few staff and no office, but able to rapidly raise hundreds of millions of dollars, it quickly led to a 'generation shift within the advocacy community'.[1] The preeminent global organisation of this kind today, Avaaz.org, claims on its website to be 'democracy in action' that is 'bringing people-powered politics to decision-making worldwide'.[2] With over 40 million members spread across the globe, it is indeed an impressive example of this new generation of civil society organisation. Its innovative and extensive use of online member participation in agenda-setting has brought participatory campaigning to a new level: it uses annual all-member polls to set overall priorities, and 10,000-member random sample emails to determine the most popular and effective campaign ideas.

On the streets, the demonstrations initiated, at least in part, by the 2010-12 Arab Spring were all predominately network protests, full of 'fluid switching between electronic and physical space, informal alliances, [and] little emphasis on hierarchy or ideology'.[3] From the protestors in Cairo's Tahrir Square to Los Indignados in Puerta del Sol in Madrid, Occupy Wall Street in Zuccotti Park, New York, and in Istanbul, São Paulo and many other places around the globe, one remarkable aspect, across all the various countries involved, was people's ability to self-organise using modern technology. Many observers struggled to come to grips with the existence of these 'leaderless revolutions', and the initial absence of the usual suspects, such as trade unions and the large, well-established civil society groups was notable. The locus of organising was often Twitter, Facebook or directly democratic assemblies during the protests. However, as Hardt and Negri note, the social media tools were used because they most closely and efficiently mimicked the new network form of struggle. These websites did not determine the structure or nature of the protest – the nature of the protest determined that these tools would be used. They were not 'Facebook revolutions'.[4] One very interesting aspect of peer-to-peer networks is that there are no such things as leaders.

These extensions of the alter-globalisation movement of the previous decades were a 21st-century, tech-savvy version of what Naomi Klein called 'a movement of movements or coalition of coalitions': a network of groups coalescing around specific events to demand change.[5] The precursor to the alter-globalisation movement was the more or less continual decline, over the course of the last several decades, of membership of political parties and trade unions. The shift away from these unitary struggles organised by a centralised leadership, to the blossoming of the diverse identity struggles, such as those of race, gender and sexuality, occurred throughout the 1960s, '70s and '80s.

In the contemporary history of protest, network structures can be seen as the most efficient way to organise social movements in a way that respects this celebration of diversity and does not subordinate difference to ideology. Aided by the emerging communication technologies, or indeed developing and coding what they needed, this form of organising first entered widespread public consciousness during the World Trade Organization (WTO) protests in Seattle in 1999. A wide variety of groups, including environmentalists, unions, church groups and other civil society organisations, came together without any central, unifying structure.[6] Indymedia, one of the most prominent forerunners of the 'Web 2.0' revolution, came of age in Seattle;

within a decade, its user-generated, participatory style had been imitated and commercialised, and turned to the more profitable purposes of shopping and advertising.

Networks have transformed how mainstream politics is done, how civil society operates and how protest unfolds. But has democracy itself been impacted? In the most trivial of senses, it has. Democracy is embedded in our changing societies – as political campaigning and protest are transformed, so too is democracy to some extent. But in another, almost as trivial sense, it has not. Democracy is still about elections and leaders and parliaments or congresses coming together to propose and vote on laws – much as it was long before the microchip was invented. As David Van Reybrouck, author of *Against Elections* and organiser of the Belgian G1000 democratic experiment mentioned below, says: 'Isn't it remarkable that innovation is the motto of our time, but that we don't apply it to our way of governing?'[7]

The more important ways democracy might change and be changed can best be contemplated with a better understanding of the core characteristics of the information revolution. Identifying and elucidating the main processes and structures will show which aspects of this revolution should be incorporated into a 21st-century democracy and which should be avoided. It will be argued that the tools, skills and processes needed to collaborate collectively and decide together exist and can be applied to fix our broken politics. This is done in the following chapters, but first we place our information age in a brief historical context.

Revolutions in communication have swept across large parts of the world before. Although both China and Korea had systems of moveable type several centuries before Europe, it was the invention of the printing press – which spread across Europe and the world in the late 15th and 16th centuries – that led to a rapid increase in the dissemination of knowledge. This was a crucial factor in the resurgence of learning, which was an integral part of the European Renaissance and Protestant Reformation.

The development of the telegraph transformed more than just communication. Its expansion throughout the 19th century, often along newly constructed railway lines or laid underwater by the recently invented steamships, for the first time decoupled long-distance communication from a material medium.[8] No longer did physical letters have to be signed, sealed and delivered over land and sea. News of what was happening in New York could get to London more or less instantaneously, instead of taking around ten days to cross the North Atlantic by ship. This revolution in communication initiated by the telegraph assisted a nascent capitalism and industrial revolution to expand to the far reaches of the globe; soon after, slavery and serfdom were (largely) banished and peasants were transformed into workers.[9]

Analogue recorded media first appeared in the late 19th and early 20th centuries in the form of photographs, movies and the phonograph. It democratised access to the arts by radically decreasing the cost of reproducing images and sounds, and in so doing undermined classical high culture by transforming it into a mass-marketed product labelled entertainment. Many artists turned to designing advertising and musicians to composing soundtracks, and the painted portrait was more often than not replaced by the photograph.[10] Nowadays, many of the smartest minds are trying to determine how to make people click more online advertisements.

The invention of the microchip and various open Internet protocols, allowing low-cost computers to be networked, is the departure point for the remaining chapters in this part. From the invention of transistors in 1947 and their integration into microchips in 1957, technology advanced rapidly. ARPANET (using the forerunner to the Internet protocols first published in 1974) was created in 1969, followed by microprocessors in 1971. The personal computer (PC) appeared in 1981 and the World Wide Web (WWW) in 1990.[11] By combining this technology with our ability to harness parts of the electromagnetic spectrum for wireless communication (first done for radio – giving the Germans an early advantage in World War I – and later for television and now mobile phones) we have even liberated these networked computers from the home and office. We can now carry access to the World Wide Web, and each other, in our pockets: the smartphone is one of the most obvious, and by now ubiquitous, recent manifestation of this revolution.[12]

As in every other communication revolution, the modern one has seen a radical increase in the quantity and speed of information flows and processing. However, today the difference in the degree of information exchange has become so large that it has become a difference in kind, allowing the development and uptake of behaviours, processes and organisational structures that were hitherto prohibitively expensive.[13]

It should be acknowledged, however, that there are dissenting voices to this narrative. Ha-Joon Chang argues that the telegraph and washing machine changed society more than the Internet, and warns that every generation thinks the changes happening in their time are more profound than those in the past.[14] He may be right. However, even if he is, it is still possible to insist that the current changes are highly significant. It is not necessary to argue that this information revolution is more (or less) rapid or profound than previous revolutions in order to undertake to understand and anticipate its outcomes, even if Castells does take up that challenge; he points out that in the US, radio took 30 years to reach 60 million people, TV took 15 years and the internet, after the invention of the WWW, took just 3 years.[15] Trying to understand the impact and importance of the modern information revolution has become an industry in itself, filling numerous books and blogs alike. An Internet search of the phrase 'information revolution' returns almost half a million results and more than 1,800 books.[16]

What is without doubt is that networks and networked processes have spread into nearly every aspect of modern life, and, when the economic transaction costs of staying connected are so low, their spread will surely continue.

So what *are* the core characteristics of these networks? They will be elaborated upon below, but briefly, in general, the networks are open, remarkably transparent, participatory and collaborative. The nodes (or participants) are largely autonomous and can therefore be highly diverse, and the products of these networks, placed in common, are often immaterial, reproducible at effectively zero cost and therefore easily shareable. Sometimes the processes involved aim to be deliberative, whereby the interactions are governed by the mutual exchange of reasons (as opposed to the issuing of commands).

These characteristics are analysed in the following chapters: the network structure in Chapter Seven, the immaterial nature of many network products in Chapter Eight, the collaborative and participatory nature of its processes in Chapter Nine, and the deliberative structure of some of its decisions in Chapter Ten.

The most popular example of these new structures and processes is probably Wikipedia, which is the only website in the top ten most popular Internet sites operated by a not-for-profit foundation. There is no doubting that Wikipedia is an impressive, transformative achievement: the ongoing, distributed and peer-reviewed improvement of the documentation of knowledge placed for free in the commons is one of the best illustrations of network collaboration made easy. Its procedures, processes and decisions are open and transparent, and it is deliberately and emphatically participatory.[17] Anyone with Internet access can click 'edit' and contribute to a Wikipedia article. Anyone can look at the 'talk' page to see why certain sentences and facts made it into an article and why others did not – and then he or she can also easily contribute to the debate.

Yet it pays to be wary. As a phenomenally successful project, Wikipedia is often used as evidence for a wide variety of theses. A good anecdote will trump the facts every time – as journalists and story-tellers well know – so it is with a degree of healthy scepticism that Wikipedia is introduced as the prime example of a network. One tree does not make a forest, and one website does not make an information revolution.

Wikipedia does, however, share many similarities with open-source software development, (ideal) academic practice and many other online 'Web 2.0' processes. The ideals are, of course, often approached imperfectly, especially outside these realms. Corporations and institutions will adopt some of the behaviours while trying to limit others, or will pay lip service to the ideals while in practice undermining them.

The important point, as far as democracy is concerned, is that the several important, overlapping core characteristics common to the most successful, productive peer networks can be interpreted positively. Autonomy can imply freedom and tolerance for diversity; peer can imply respect and equality; participation can imply belonging and deliberation can imply moral outcomes.

These outcomes are, however, far from automatic. As will be shown, networks are not always or necessarily progressive – indeed, they also, almost paradoxically, lead to inequality in closed, biased and hierarchical groups. Further exploration of these common features, and their positive and negative aspects, is warranted. How to structure a network to mesh the positive qualities with good deliberative processes, and achieve legitimate democratic decision-making, is the challenge addressed in Part Three.

Notes

1. Dave Karpf, *The MoveOn Effect: Disruptive Innovation within the Interest*

Group Ecology of American Politics, https://davekarpf.files.wordpress.com/2009/03/moveon.pdf. This was later expanded into a book.

2. https://www.avaaz.org/page/en/.

3. Quote is from Andy Beckett's book review of Paul Mason's *Why It's Kicking Off Everywhere*. See: https://www.theguardian.com/books/2012/jan/11/kicking-off-everywhere-paul-mason-review.

4. Michael Hardt and Antonio Negri, *Declaration* (Kindle e-book edition, 2012), 4.

5. http://www.pbs.org/wgbh/commandingheights/shared/pdf/int_naomiklein.pdf. 'Alter-globalisation' is a term used by protestors who reject the label 'anti-globalisation': they do not demand a halt to globalisation but want a different kind of globalisation.

6. Hardt and Negri, *Multitude*, 217.

7. Benoît Derenne *et al.*, *G1000 Final Report: Democratic Innovation in Practice* (2012), 95, http://www.g1000.org/documents/G1000_EN_Website.pdf.

8. The point here is that a physical object bearing the message no longer had to be transported from one place to another. All communication – even radio and wireless internet – of course relies on some medium (such as electromagnetic waves), but the 'decoupling' refers to how messages were no longer constrained by the need to transport an object physically.

9. Hobsbawm, *Capital*, 48: 'the telegraph… finally represented the means of communication adequate to modern means of production'; and 216: 'Three types of agrarian enterprise were under particular pressure: the slave plantation, the serf estate, and the traditional non-capitalist peasant economy'.

10. Hobsbawm, *Extremes*, Chapter Seventeen, and 513.

11. Castells, *Information*, vol. 1, 40.

12. The invention of fast-charging, lightweight batteries was also a crucial part of this development.

13. Shirky, *Everybody*, 149.

14. Ha-Joon Chang, *23 Things They Don't Tell You About Capitalism* (Allen Lane, 2010), 37.

15. Castells, *Information*, vol. 1, 382.

16. Searching for 'information revolution' (in quotes) on http://www.google.com, and in the book section of http://amazon.com, performed on 8 November 2015.

17. This is an overly simplistic outline of how Wikipedia works. For more details, including the various levels of privilege and access bestowed on certain users, see Phoebe Ayers, Charles Matthews and Ben Yates, *How Wikipedia Works: And How You Can Be Part of It* (No Starch Press, 2008).

Chapter 7: Flattening Hierarchies

The first and most obvious common characteristic of the elements of the current information revolution is the peer-to-peer network form.

In abstract terms, a network is a structure consisting of nodes connected by many links, like a collection of circles, some of which are joined to each other by lines. The nodes can be, for example, people, computers, cities or websites, and the links could be friendships, wires, roads or hyperlinks.

A *peer* network is one where the nodes both consume from and supply resources to other nodes without any centralised coordination. This makes it impossible to attribute what is produced by such a network to any one node, and invariably means that the actions or products are made freely available to everyone in the network, and often even to nodes outside of it. Such products are said to be placed in the public *commons*. Who is the author of a Wikipedia article? It is impossible to say; ownership has no meaning when so many people contribute to any particular article.

Social (but not family) life has always been typically structured by peers acting in networks. Facebook, blogs, Twitter and the rest are simply free or low-cost, easy-to-use manifestations of our general networking behaviour, although the extent of their spread and the number of connections take the flow of information to an entirely new level. Social media is not only redefining the concept of friendship, it is redefining how friends interact, how (and how fast) ideas spread through social networks (and occasionally go viral), and how people organise and structure non-work time. Every event in life becomes potential content, and distributed networks of acquaintances can all participate, albeit to a limited extent, in sharing the experience.

For the purposes of this book, a network is defined as a number of autonomous nodes (or people) collaborating to provide a product or service that none could provide alone as efficiently. They are essentially interdependent, and as there is no centralised command directing the actions of the others, their structure is considered horizontal as opposed to hierarchical. There is no one telling the contributors to a Wikipedia article what to do, no one directing your interactions on Facebook and no one telling open-source software developers where to focus their development and bug-fixing efforts. In any of these sufficiently large networks the sudden removal of any particular node, or even several of them, will not overly disrupt the network as a whole. This is not, in general, the case in a hierarchy, where the sudden loss of several key people in a command structure could significantly affect its performance.

In his monumental three-volume study of the rise of the network society, Manuel Castells traces the consolidation of what he calls the 'horizontal corporation' or the 'network enterprise' back to the 1980s.[1] Historically, the use of explicit hierarchies in business was led by the large US railway corporations in the 1800s. They imported the command-and-control systems of the military and state bureaucracies to avoid being overwhelmed by the information processing necessary to coordinate the complex movement of trains across the entire country.[2] Deliberately limiting the flow of information by insulating layers of managers from each other and from the workers, each with clearly defined and routinised tasks, solved what Clay Shirky calls 'the institutional dilemma' of how to minimise the transaction costs associated with managing large numbers of people. It became the benchmark organisational structure of Fordism – assembly-line production was the manifestation of this idea on factory floors.[3]

In the 1980s, a few prescient business leaders came to believe that the old command-and-control management model was outdated. The costs of complex processing and communication of information had declined significantly and hierarchies were perceived as being too rigid to respond profitably to the rapidly changing economic, technological and institutional environment. Changes were instigated to enhance flexibility in production, management and marketing; the suppression, or flattening, of managerial layers and corporate hierarchies was an important part of this process. The shift to networked labour began, and soon intensified. In industries from finance to engineering to design, employees were required to act with a high degree of relative autonomy and creativity within a network of peers.[4]

Indeed, today, profitable traders, researchers and software developers are valuable because they are deeply embedded in a wide network of knowledge sources and personal contacts. The expertise is distributed across a network of cooperating, autonomous and creative individuals and experts, and knowledge, which in general becomes *common* (or shared) knowledge, is most efficiently produced by interactions spread across the network. Often such networks are highly social, and will exist beyond the bounds of any one company; they can also include academics, government bureaucrats and members of civil society. When several of the world's biggest currency traders were dealt record fines in 2014, the investigation detailed how 'Traders at different banks formed tight-knit groups in which information was shared about client activity.'[5] Although the network structure is obvious, a high degree of individual autonomy is also apparent when massive losses can be incurred by various rogue traders.

The spread of these network ideals has increased the levels of precarity, flexibility and mobility in many jobs.[6] It has blurred the distinction between work and non-work time, especially as the development of social relationships is a key component. The division of work has become between a core of 'information-based managers... and a *disposable labor force* that can be automated and/or hired/fired/offshored depending on market demand and labor costs' (emphasis in original).[7] Network structures came to permeate even those sectors of the economy dealing with physical goods.

Interestingly, Castells claims that 'organizational changes interacted with the diffusion of information technology but by and large were independent, and in general preceded the diffusion of information technologies in business firms'.[8] It was a chicken-and-egg situation: organisational form and technology converged, and arguing which came first is perhaps a futile debate.

What lessons for democracy can be derived from the rise of network structures? Perhaps the most important lesson is a negative one, stemming from the important distinction between a hierarchical *structure* and inequalities of power and influence. The structure of a network is one where there are relatively few restrictions on the connectivity or flow of information. In a hierarchy, by contrast, such restrictions are deliberately imposed: each node takes commands from only one node further up the hierarchy, and issues commands to those nodes directly subordinate to it. Power, in a formal hierarchy, is clearly defined. However, across a network, the distribution of resources and power will typically also be highly unequal. Some nodes will be larger, or have more connections or resources, or be more influential than other nodes.

On Wikipedia, the large number of participants include a vast majority who contribute little and a small few who contribute much. Even though Wikipedia is open to any contributor, in practice formal and informal hierarchies emerge when a small fraction of people, generally male, make the lion's share of contributions. Wikipedia is far from egalitarian, and this tendency has apparently increased with the emergence of stable groups of high-level editors with permissions and influence that the large number of occasional contributors do not have. It is also interesting that many other projects placed on other wikis (which are simply easy-to-use, collaborative, online document-production tools) often fail – the tool must be accompanied by a dedicated community striving towards a broadly shared purpose, and it would seem the chance of success is helped if that purpose is not profit *per se*, but for some wider social benefit.

Nearly every measure of Internet participation and connectivity follows this power-law distribution, where much effort, influence or attention is concentrated in a few nodes or people, accompanied by a long tail of many who do little. The blogosphere is a space of millions of little-followed blogs and relatively few highly subscribed sites. Ditto for Facebook and YouTube: the collection of pages or videos with millions of likes is a minuscule fraction of the entire set.

This differs fundamentally from entities whose distributions follow a typical Gaussian 'bell curve', as is the case for human height. Whereas for a bell curve you can meaningfully talk about norms and averages, there is no such thing as normal in a network.

Inequalities of power and influence invariably exist within all networks, and in this sense every network will typically have a 'hierarchical' distribution of power, even if they are not formally, or structurally, hierarchical. As Shirky is at pains to highlight, networks are 'NOT [a] posthierarchical paradise'.[9] Equality, one of the key principles of democracy, is not something you often find in networks; networks are rarely democratic.

Nor is there anything implicit in the structure of peer-to-peer networks that guarantees freedom, legitimacy, empowerment or any other such lofty ideal. Global power is now expressed through a network of 'dominant nation states along with supranational institutions, major capitalist corporations, and other powers'.[10] As mentioned above, in the workplace the network form was conceived and implemented to make workers more responsive to the economic needs of the corporation, blurring the distinction between work and non-work time, and seeking to increase worker flexibility or, in other words, to reduce security, demand more mobility of workers and make it easier to hire and fire them.[11] State power is now increasingly network power, and John Dryzek documents the transition 'from Demos to Network, from Government to Governance', warning that 'electoral democracy is in trouble when networked governance dominates', since there is no obvious accountability mechanism or well-defined counter-power in a network.[12]

The old media behemoths may be in the process of being

dethroned, but they have been replaced by the new digital behemoths of Google and Facebook, which have a far more pervasive, and potentially pernicious, access to the details of our lives. Advertising revenue is flooding to these channels, and what constitutes news is also being redefined: truth and quality are being sacrificed to virality – digital business models are based on the number of clicks a story gets, which has little to do with accuracy, relevance or importance.[13] It is open to debate whether drowning in attention-absorbing clickbait stifles dissent less than authoritarian regimes' typical preference for restricting access to it.[14]

Sharing networks such as Airbnb and Uber may be cheap and convenient, but they are making a profit by undermining industries where workers have fought hard for rights, benefits and minimum wages. The 'workforce' of people driving for Uber or cleaning Airbnb apartments are probably not members of any union. In fact, they are not employees but contractors – with no holiday pay, no sick leave or maternity leave, or any other typical worker benefits (although this is being challenged in the courts). 'In modern times we have been miseducated to believe that consumer choice is all-powerful, but the idea that consumers exercising their sovereign right to choose will always lead to the best outcomes is obviously in the interests of corporations seeking to escape official regulation,' says Steven Poole, reviewing Tom Slee's book *What's Yours is Mine: Against the Sharing Economy*.[15] Networks are not democratic, and network production is not necessarily progressive.

Equality does not arise spontaneously in a network; the reverse is probably true, since networks seem predisposed to inequality and imbalances in power. Not that equality and networks are mutually exclusive either. As will be shown in Part Three, it is *not* difficult to construct a network of equals. However, to institute such a network form of democracy it should be anticipated that the network will necessarily be a highly artificial one – tightly constrained to induce and enforce democratic equality.

Notes

1. Castells, *Information*, vol. 1, 165. See also, for example, David Harvey, *The Condition of Postmodernity: An Enquiry into the Origins of Cultural Change* (Basil Blackwell, 1989), especially Chapter Nine, 'From Fordism to Flexible Accumulation'.

2. Shirky, *Everybody*, 40–2; Hobsbawm, *Capital*, 254–5.

3. 'Fordism' is named after Henry Ford (1863–1947), the founder of the Ford Motor Company, who was one of the first to introduce assembly lines in the mass production of cars.

4. Castells, *Information*, vol. 1, 257.

5. Jill Treanor, 'Record Fines for Forex Rigging', *Guardian Weekly*, 21 November 2014.

6. Castells, *Information*, vol. 1, 302.

7. Castells, *Information*, 295–6.

8. Castells, *Information*, 165, but see also 166–87.

9. Shirky, *Everybody*, 23.

10. Hardt and Negri, *Multitude*, xii. This was the principal point of their book, *Empire*. Or, more awkwardly, in Keane, *Democracy*, 781: 'joined-up global government'.

11. Hardt and Negri, *Multitude*, 65–6.

12. Dryzek with Niemeyer, *Foundations*, 119, 123, and indeed most of Chapter Six, 'Governance Networks'.

13. Katharine Viner, 'Technology's Disruption of the Truth', *Guardian Weekly*, 22 July 2016.

14. Hardt and Negri, *Declaration*, 14.

15. Steven Poole, 'Winners and Sharers', *Guardian Weekly*, 29 April 2016.

Chapter 8: The Production of No-thing

It is often the case that the products of networks and their processes, such as information or an information-processing algorithm, are *immaterial*. They have no material existence. You can neither touch information nor smell an algorithm. If the first core characteristic of the information revolution is its network structure, the immaterial nature of many of its products is the second.

The laws that govern us are, if nothing else, also immaterial – they are a complex set of rules and procedures. As such, they should be highly amenable to network processes, but before exploring what the immaterial nature of network production might mean for democracy it is instructive to understand how it has transformed modern corporations.

Information and knowledge have always been important to industry, and a principal source of wealth, but what is different now is how they have rapidly become not only important but crucial aspects of corporate profits. As Castells states: 'Information technologies make it possible for information itself to become the product of the production process. To be more precise: the products of new information-technology industries are information-processing devices or information processing itself.'[1] Data is the new oil. But, as with oil, it is only a primary input to the production process. What is up for sale today is often not *what* is produced from information but *how* it is produced. Algorithms, typically in the form of computer software, perform computations to transform data and produce more information, and although the new information may be marketable, it is the holders of the algorithms who often make the truly staggering profits.

It is estimated that well over half of all trading on US stock markets is being done by algorithms that automatically buy and sell stocks based on the real-time predictions of complex mathematical models.[2] These quantitative trading algorithms (or 'quants') can make millions of transactions each second, and this high-frequency trading has been implicated in the stock market 'flash crash' of 6 May 2010, when the Dow Jones tumbled and lost trillions of dollars in just a few minutes, before regaining itself minutes later. At a more mundane level, your local supermarket has programs tracking and analysing every purchase to determine shopping habits, the most effective placement of products, stock ordering and delivery. Software is now everywhere.

The integration of networked devices and processing is an integral aspect of the rapid expansion of financial capitalism, the push to outsourcing, crowdsourcing, just-in-time delivery, cloud computing and Wikipedia, and much more besides.

As Castells observes, it is 'not the centrality of knowledge and information, but the application of knowledge and information to knowledge generation and information processing/communication devices' that is of fundamental importance in the informational society.[3] It is the *process*, rather than the output, that is often the primary product. Moreover, these algorithmic, immaterial processes and products do not obey the logic of scarcity that applies to finite, material products. Algorithms can be copied and shared at practically zero cost and without limit – which is why, as much as music and film producers try to insist otherwise, copying and breach of copyright are fundamentally different from stealing. Even if they may both be against the law, and may both reduce the profits of corporations, copying – unlike stealing – does not deny use to anyone else. If someone steals a chair, no one else can sit on it, but copying a file or software program has no effect on the original owner or program.

Restricting access to such easily reproducible entities is often difficult, and is seen as counterproductive by open-source software developers.[4] In open-source software development, profit is extracted at a different point: by offering support, services and extensions while participating in and relying on the open, distributed development of what are essentially infinitely and easily reproducible, complex algorithms.

In the last few decades, there has been extraordinary growth in entire sectors of the economy dealing for the most part in these immaterial products and their related services: software programs, digital films and music, financial derivatives and products, currency trades and treasury bonds, brands and trademarks, genetic sequences, biochemical and other patents and copyrights, intellectual property, and so on. A significant part of the workforce is now employed to develop, maintain and sell products that in their final form are reproducible almost for free as they have virtually no material existence except, perhaps, as a thin layer of magnetised material on a hard-disk drive.[5]

Castells talks of 'a fundamental process of restructuring of the capitalist system from the 1980s onwards' with 'the rise of informationalism', which has induced 'a pattern of discontinuity in the material basis of the economy, society and culture'.[6] In other words, things have changed, fast. Although Castells's preferred description is 'informational society' – as a contrast to the prior industrial and agrarian societies – he rejects the label 'post-industrial' as he posits that the new structures have not so much replaced or superseded these prior modes of production as they have completely transformed and extended them, so that we should now talk about info-industrial and info-agricultural production.[7] He provides a wealth of data and examples, such as the application of patented genetics to agriculture, and electronics and computational processing to industry, to show how they have both been thoroughly permeated by the new processes and technologies. The 'productivity and competitiveness of units or agents in this [informational] economy (be it firms, regions or nations) fundamentally depend upon their capacity to generate, process and apply efficiently knowledge-based information,' he says.[8] This transformation occurred hand in hand with the incredible development and expansion of the more obviously informational industries such as finance and computing; finance (including insurance) now often produces one-fifth of the annual profits in highly developed capitalist states.[9]

Hardt and Negri see all these changes stemming directly from the 'paradigm of immaterial production', whose central aspect is its 'intimate relation with cooperation, collaboration, and communication – in short, its foundation in the common'.[10] The Fordist model of business organisation has been displaced and the dominant production ideal has become the network structure:

> The contemporary scene of labor and production... is being transformed under the hegemony of immaterial labor, that is, labor that produces immaterial products, such as information, knowledge, ideas, images, relationships, and affects. This does not mean that there is no more industrial working class whose calloused hands toil with machines or that there are no more agricultural workers who till the soil. It does not even mean that the numbers of such workers have decreased globally. In fact, workers involved primarily in immaterial production are a small minority of the global whole. What it means, rather, is that the qualities and characteristics of immaterial production are tending to transform the other forms of labor and indeed society as a whole... [I]mmaterial labor tends to take the social form of networks based on communication, collaboration, and affective relationships. Immaterial

labor can only be conducted in common, and increasingly immaterial labor invents new, independent networks of cooperation through which it produces. Its ability to engage and transform all aspects of society and its collaborative network form are two enormously powerful characteristics that immaterial labor is spreading to other forms of labor.[11]

This will be crucial for a transformed democracy. Our laws are immaterial, and if the ideal of network production of immaterial objects is spreading, then its spread to democracy can be encouraged and supported.

University academics, whose primary product – knowledge – is essentially immaterial, represent the archetype of a peer-to-peer network environment. Indeed, much of the infrastructure underlying the current communications revolution – for example, computers, the Internet, email and the World Wide Web – was either first invented, or at least extensively used and further developed, by and for academics, researchers from large electronics corporations and the military. Throughout the 1970s and '80s, these tools were used almost exclusively by these professionals, and were rapidly adopted further afield because they dramatically lowered the costs of distributed collaboration and the complex processing of information.[12] Before the information revolution, most successful scientists were already embedded in research networks and collaborative projects; afterwards, these networks became incredibly easy to establish, maintain and extend, and grew far more efficient.

It is perhaps not surprising that the system for processing the knowledge produced by academics is called peer review, whereby results are published only if an academic's peers deem the work acceptable. The approval process is dispersed across the network; and the results are published in journals for all in the network to see.[13]

Academics, in several well-publicised cases of participatory 'Citizen Science', have even crowdsourced part of the research effort. Kevin Schawinski, one of the founding scientists of one renowned example, Galaxy Zoo, described the network of 250,000 volunteers as 'the world's most powerful pattern-recognising super-computer, [which] existed in the linked intelligence of all the people who logged on to our website: and this global brain was processing this stuff incredibly fast and incredibly accurately. It was extraordinary.'[14]

With Galaxy Zoo, although the scientific results may be impressive, it is the activity that is newsworthy. Similarly, for Wikipedia, although it is the articles on the website that everyone finds useful, it is neither them nor the tool being used (the wiki) that makes Wikipedia a *truly* remarkable project: it is the community of people dedicating their time to improve the content. Above all, 'a Wikipedia article is a process, not a product, and as a result, it is never finished... [I]t replaces guarantees offered by institutions with probabilities supported by process', says Shirky.[15] And it works. Scientific articles in the English version are regularly rated as good as the articles produced by experts for *Encyclopaedia Britannica*.[16]

It is certainly an impressive example of what Castells means when he states:

> New information technologies are not simply tools to be applied, but processes to be developed. Users and doers may become the same... For the first time in history, the human mind is a direct productive force, not just a decisive element of the production system... What we think, and how we think, become expressed in goods, services, material and intellectual output.[17]

Hardt and Negri prefer to use the term *performance*: 'Every form of labor that produces an immaterial good... is fundamentally a performance: the product is the act itself.'[18] Everyone who is reading a Wikipedia article can edit that article, and the process (performance) of arguing for or against a proposed edit is an essential component of the article.

In short, peer-to-peer networks are well suited to processes that produce non-exclusive, easily shareable, immaterial products placed in common.

What does this imply for democracy?

One crucial realisation, and one of the original inspirations for this book, is that the laws that govern us are precisely the kind of immaterial product that are, in theory, perfectly suited to production through a modern peer-to-peer, deliberative and open network. Could all the laws that bind us be placed on a wiki – perhaps called WikiPolicy, WikiLaws or WikiGovernment – along with a history of the changes made to them? What would happen if everyone and anyone could propose, discuss and deliberate on suggested changes?[19] What laws would emerge from such a networked process? A limited version of such an experiment has been performed: it is called

Wikipedia. In an interesting example of self-reference, Wikipedia collaboration is itself governed by multiple policies specifying the 'rules of operation' that are themselves other Wikipedia pages subject to similar deliberative, collaborative processes as the 'article' pages.[20] If you think a Wikipedia policy should be different, you can propose changes, argue your point and participate in the same way as with the articles.

Policy development on a wiki has also been attempted within at least one political party. The Green Party of Western Australia set up a wiki prior to the 2008 Western Australian state election, open to any member of the party, and used it for several years thereafter to develop and discuss state party policy.

It is reasonably easy to dismiss the objection that the intricate legal language of laws and their complex interdependence would render any WikiLaw project infeasible. In the current parliamentary system, although laws are ultimately written by teams of legal experts, this is theoretically a largely technical process. These lawyers are tasked with translating the wishes and desires of the government of the day into legal jargon – it is the detailed outline of policy positions (in widely comprehensible terms) that could be captured by such a wiki-process.

The principal objection to such a process stems directly from the inequalities of power inherent in networks mentioned above. Those with time, energy, technical expertise and the passion and motivation could easily dominate such processes. As already stated, inequalities will generally be exacerbated in an open network. So what kind of participation would a democratic network creating immaterial laws require? It is to this question that we now turn.

Notes

1. Castells, *Information*, vol. 1, 30, 70–1, 78.

2. Charles Arthur, 'The Dangers of Big Data', *Guardian Weekly*, 30 August 2013.

3. Castells, *Information*, vol. 1, 31.

4. Hardt and Negri, *Multitude*, 311.

5. Google's core service, its search engine, makes the 'crowd' of websites navigable through the application of its immaterial algorithms (such as its famous patented PageRank algorithm). Even traditional bricks-and-mortar companies, such as Walmart, now sell life insurance and develop projects, such as the 'Social

Genome Project' of @WalmartLabs, which mines data from Facebook and other social media sites to better target products and advertising. For Walmart, see http://www.huffingtonpost.com/al-norman/the-walmartfacebook-socia_b_1714802.html.

6. Castells, *Information*, vol. 1, 13, 14, 29.

7. Castells, *Information*, 218–26 refers to the 'myth' of the post-industrial society. See also Chang, *23 Things*, 92, 93, 96; and Hobsbawm, *Extremes*, 302–4.

8. Castells, *Information*, vol. 1, 77.

9. It was the development of the technologies of transactions that virtually eliminated transaction costs in finance, making the high-frequency trading by algorithms commonplace, and allowing capital to flow around the planet with exceptional ease – capital mobility being a major source of the higher returns reaped by holders of immaterial financial assets. 'Throughout the 1980s there was a massive technological investment in the communications/information infrastructure that made possible the twin movements of deregulation of markets and globalization of capital,' says Castells, *Information*, vol. 1, 97; see also 102 and especially Table 2.6. The industry has further created an impressive array of immaterial financial products, such as derivatives and credit default swaps, which can only exist because computers can price, track and manage them. Tax havens play a crucial role in the industry: companies transferring high-value intangible assets, such as brands and intellectual property rights, to tax havens have been targeted by campaigners and governments alike. See also Patrick Wintour and Simon Bowers, 'G20 Backs Radical Action on Tax Evasion', *Guardian Weekly*, 26 July 2013.

10. Hardt and Negri, *Multitude*, 174. See also 54, 81 for more on networks, communication, collaboration and interaction; 108 about affective labour; 113 about how the control and production of information has become dominant; and 114 for the growing importance of intellectual property rights and other evidence.

11. Hardt and Negri, *Multitude*, 65–6. See also 107–8 for an elaboration on hegemony as a tendency and more on the characteristics of immaterial labour; and 114–15 for a 'reality check' for evidence of this hegemony.

12. Castells, *Information*, vol. 1, 17: 'Informationalism is oriented [its 'performance principle' or measure of success]… toward the accumulation of knowledge and towards higher levels of complexity in information processing'.

13. Many other transformations are rippling through academia: the 'open science' movement has called for a shift from the public publication of academic results to the open publication of results, often in free online journals such as those of the Public Library of Science. From medicine to astronomy, researchers are heeding the call for 'open data for open science' and sharing raw data freely; OpenCourseWare, the free online publication of university course material for anyone to peruse, and Open Universities (the first of which appeared in the UK), with little to no restrictions on admissions to undergraduate courses, are enabling easier access to education. 'Peer instruction' entails students discussing 'concept tests' in small groups to collectively develop understanding, and Massive Open Online Courses (MOOCs) extend this concept online. Interactive classes that use peer review and assessment, like those of EdX, have attracted hundreds of thousands of students to individual courses (even if typically far fewer complete the course). At this level of participation, it is impossible for a lecturer to assist students to develop understanding, or undertake the task of assessment: networks of students do both. See, for example, the Public Library of Science: http://www.plos.org/; Michael Nielson, *Reinventing Discovery: The New Era of*

Networked Science (Princeton University Press, 2011); Ian Sample, 'DNA Data to be Shared Worldwide for Medical Research', *Guardian Weekly*, 21 June 2013; http://crts.caltech.edu/ – Astronomers released the entire dataset from their Catalina Sky Survey, stating: 'In the era of an exponential data growth, it is silly to be data-selfish: not any one group can do it all on their own. Sharing data is good.' Eric Mazur, *Peer Instruction: A User's Manual* (Prentice Hall, 1997).

14. Tim Adams, 'Galaxy Zoo', *Guardian Weekly*, 30 March 2012. See also http://en.wikipedia.org/wiki/Galaxy_Zoo quotes of the 2 August 2007, Galaxy Zoo newsletter. See also http://www.zooniverse.org/.

15. Shirky, *Everybody*, 119, 139.

16. Jim Giles, 'Internet Encyclopaedias Go Head to Head', *Nature*, 2005, Vol. 438, 900–1.

17. Castells, *Information*, vol. 1, 31.

18. Hardt and Negri, *Multitude*, 200.

19. Beth Simone Noveck, *Wiki Government: How Technology Can Make Government Better, Democracy Stronger, and Citizens More Powerful* (Brookings Institution Press, 2009).

20. See, for example, https://en.wikipedia.org/wiki/Wikipedia:Policies_and_guidelines.

Chapter 9: Participate!

Another obvious potentially positive trait of efficient peer-to-peer networks is that they are often transparent and open, and encourage participation, cooperation and collaboration. On Wikipedia, anyone who respects the process is free to join and contribute to an article. The network is deliberately participatory, encouraging people to engage their own unique skills in progressing the project. From a simple activity such as correcting the grammar in a Wikipedia article, commenting on blogs or posting on Facebook, to the more skilled activities of fixing bugs or adding features to a piece of open-source software such as WordPress, tools and communities exist to facilitate and support participation. In some networks, the bar is placed higher before participation is allowed. Submissions to academic journals are, in general, restricted to academics and researchers from relevant institutions. However, every person who is qualified can, in principle, participate by submitting an article.

It is not that the voluntary participants in many of these networks are altruists. Open-source software developers fix bugs because their income depends on being able to supply and support customers with a good product. Academics review other academics' papers (often for free) not only to participate in an essential part of the academic process, but also to be the first to learn about new research, and because it is a mark of respect to be requested to do so.

Cooperative, participatory networks have always existed. In primates and other social mammals, although dominance hierarchies often exist, a vast array of coordinated networking capabilities is displayed when hunting, grooming, sharing food or defending territory. Every human is embedded in multiple, complex layers of kin, colleague and friendship networks and their related channels and ways of communicating and cooperating: 'Evidence from evolutionary biology and psychology, anthropology and game theory shows our uniquely sophisticated capacity for co-operation is at the heart of our evolutionary success. Science is telling us we are co-operators,' says Charles Leadbeater.[1] Collaboration and cooperation are in many contexts commonplace and often taken for granted, and the definition of capitalist markets as competitive hides the obvious fact that it is internal cooperation that makes any corporation a viable entity.[2]

What is different now is that the costs of finding, forming and maintaining collaborative participatory networks of like-minded people have lowered dramatically. Seb Paquet calls it an age of 'ridiculously easy' group formation.[3] Clay Shirky points out that:

> We are living in the middle of a remarkable increase in our ability to share, to cooperate with one another, and to take collective action, all outside the framework of traditional institutions and organisations... Social tools don't create collective action – they merely remove obstacles to it. Those obstacles have been so significant and pervasive, however, that as they are being removed, the world is becoming a different place.[4]

Collaboration, participation and cooperation have also, according to Hardt and Negri above, become the hegemonic ideal. Many businesses are striving to develop and profit from the capabilities of collaborative networks and emulate the profitable practices of the corporations producing immaterial goods. Facebook and all the aspiring social media sites are the most obvious companies whose business model relies on profiting from processing the detailed information extracted from its network of users and their interactions. As other corporations seek to emulate these ideals and practices, they are contributing to the transformation to the informational, participatory society.

Many corporations have struggled to adapt to the participatory culture that has taken root. Traditional media, such as newspapers, books, films, photography, music, radio and television, are probably the industries most obviously affected by the profound shift to the participatory peer-to-peer mode of production, distribution and consumption. Many are floundering as they are rapidly challenged by companies whose core ability is often a process for networking distributed activity, which usually relies on the development and maintenance of complex computer software. Newspaper sales have plummeted as blogging expands exponentially, with sites like the Huffington Post developing the platform and processes to aggregate blog posts and news stories from diverse sources. As people switch to online news sources, advertisers have followed.[5] Photos, music, books and encyclopaedias have all gone digital, pushing entire analogue industries into collapse or severe strain. The core activity of both eBay and Amazon is the maintenance of peer-to-peer software platforms (Amazon initially for selling books, now for selling almost anything), and when the international book retailer Borders turned over its online sales to Amazon it arguably instigated its own demise. Pixar, Netflix and Flickr are all, at heart, software companies. The former was bought by Disney, the second eviscerated video rental chain Blockbuster and the third rode the wave of digital photography that brought about the downfall of Kodak.[6] Increasing numbers of people – especially the younger 'digital natives' – get more of their diet of news and entertainment online: for the first time since the invention of television, children are watching less than previous generations (but of course far more YouTube, where they can also upload their own content). In book publishing, companies such as Unbound (the publisher of this work) and John Hunt Publishing use software as a core part of their processes; for Unbound it is crowd-funding software, for John Hunt a system that networks authors together as peers in the editorial and production processes.

Many professionals in traditional media are understandably nervous. The tools and processes now exist for a network (or 'the crowd') to perform the filtering function previously done by editors, music labels and journalists. Instead of 'filter-then-publish', we have what Shirky calls the 'mass amateurization' of publishing – anyone can now publish and let the crowd perform the editorial function of filtering.[7] News can be aggregated by 'likes', newsfeeds replaced by Twitter feeds and trending hashtags, and view counts used to promote popular music and short films; some of the most recent bestselling physical books started out as prodigiously shared and downloaded e-books.[8]

None of this is possible without the participation of vast numbers of people – participation is the new norm.

The invention of three-dimensional printing paves the way for similar changes in the production of many physical entities: their distribution will be decoupled from a material medium, just as the telegraph first did for messages around 200 years ago. Getting a chair from the other side of the planet may soon become as easy as downloading the instructions and printing the chair, much to the dismay of its original designers and producers – unless the original designers are a distributed network of collaborators who need cheap chairs for some other profitable project.

Often the protocols for engaging in these networks are open and transparent, which lowers the barriers to participation. Even in the making of a car, it is no longer the case that raw materials arrive at the factory door and finished cars leave through the gate. A large network of collaborating suppliers builds the many required parts, which other suppliers integrate into various sub-assemblies, and even the final assembly-line construction can now be outsourced to contract manufacturers that also assemble cars for the competitors.[9] The rules of engagement in the network are well defined by contract law, and any appropriately equipped supplier can, in principle, attempt to participate in the network.

Open-source software is also often given as a prime example of participatory network collaboration that has challenged the traditional business model of significant parts of the computer software industry. Many people may be surprised to learn that free and open-source software runs the majority of web servers (which send you website pages when you browse the Internet), and that all three of the most popular content-management systems for websites are free and open source (WordPress, Joomla! and Drupal).[10]

All Wikipedia content, and the majority of the content of the Public Library of Science, is published under a Creative Commons licence. The specific purpose of these licences, which were inspired by the GNU General Public License developed by the Free Software Foundation for open-source computer software, is to enable and encourage open sharing, collaboration, participation and reuse.

Many further examples of the shift towards networked and participatory structures could be given. From participative art (Art 2.0), urban design, alternative currencies (Bitcoin and the distributed database structure called a 'blockchain' used to track Bitcoin exchanges), to loans (Zopa peer-to-peer lending), illicit drug-making and peer support workers in mental health, groups of people are experimenting with peer collaboration and participation.[11] All the 'Web 2.0' sites where participatory, user-generated content dominates, such as YouTube, Facebook and Twitter, would be nothing without the content placed on them for free by their users, and would not be used if they did not process and return that information in useful ways.

All these participatory websites blur the line between producer and consumer: the creation of content goes hand in hand with its consumption, and has led to the coining of the neologism 'prosumer'. Music sites such as Spotify let users collaboratively rank, organise and suggest music (or does it for them based on their listening history) and album sales are falling steadily – the music playlist is in the ascendant.

This collaborative economy has also been joined by collaborative consumption.[12] From car and bike sharing to toy libraries and community tool sheds, the move away from exclusive ownership is on the increase. The examples are far too numerous to list, but include

Streetbank, Nextdoor, Couchsurfing, Airbnb and Uber. The latter two have upset the hotel and taxi industries respectively, leading to legal challenges and protests in several countries. A common element across many of these networking sites, including Amazon, eBay and the like, is the use of reviews and ratings by participants. Credibility, in this informational age, becomes one of the most valuable resources.

Participation can, of course, be one area where governments, at least, dissemble. Governments of all stripes claim to be responsive to people's needs, so organising forums and participatory sessions open to the public is commonplace. The outcome of such exercises, however, is often taken merely as advice, and so the cynical portrayal of them as mere window-dressing for politicians to do what they want is common. It is relatively easy to consult, and it is almost as easy to ignore the results – or to pick and choose only those suggestions that chime with existing policy. The solution, as practised by groups such as the newDemocracy Foundation in Australia, is to insist beforehand that such forums will be empowered: that the outcomes will become policy or, at the very least, be subject to a free and unconstrained debate and subsequent vote in parliament (or other relevant decision-making body). This question of empowerment will be further addressed in Part Three.

One problem with open participation is that people and groups become subject to the well-established phenomenon of confirmatory bias: people tend to filter out information that conflicts with their established views, ending up in 'information cocoons'.[13] Especially online, the self-selecting nature of groups can easily result in insulation and the formation of an echo chamber where narrow views of the world are reinforced. Although access to the Internet could, 'in principle, make everyone a cosmopolitan, in practice it does nothing of the kind'.[14] The early advocates of the power of the Internet to widen minds through access to diverse sources of information have been proven wrong; we filter out what we do not want to hear. Google apparently encourages this phenomenon by altering search results based on the prior search history and user profile it constructs from your online activity: a business executive may see a different set of results to a search of 'climate change' than an environmental activist.[15] Facebook is even worse: it feeds you more of what you like, meaning you may rarely be exposed to anything on Facebook that may challenge your view of the world and what you consider interesting. So it is important not to make the Panglossian presumption that increased participation and the freedom of the network are necessarily positive; it must be acknowledged that, perhaps paradoxically, ease of participation can, in many instances, also lead to division and extremism.

The self-selecting nature of open participation is the cause of many of the problems. When Barack Obama launched his open, participatory, online, suggest-and-vote *Citizen's Briefing Book* (part of Change.gov before he became president) it was overwhelmed by the marijuana legalisation lobby and its supporters. Proposals for marijuana legalisation managed to top the list of questions in nearly every category, including health and economics. When the UK's Natural Environment Research Council suggest-and-vote process ended up with a clear win for 'Boaty McBoatface' as the most popular name for its new polar research vessel, they ultimately selected the respectable fifth-placed name, skipping even the fourth place suggestion of 'It's bloody cold here'.[16] The problem of self-selection is also evident on Wikipedia, where the majority of editors are male. Participation in open groups and networks is never guaranteed to be *representative* participation.

Similar problems arose in the 2011 social movements. The open assemblies at Occupy Wall Street, where protestors made their decisions, were understandably inspiring to many who initially experienced them. Seeing participatory democracy in action, where everyone is afforded respect and the time to contribute, directly counters the powerlessness experienced by people in normal politics. Unfortunately, assemblies such as these, more often than not, do not endure. It is not a pretty spectacle to see such assemblies degenerate into decision-making by attrition, whereby only those persistent or passionate enough to persevere until the bitter end contribute to decisions. Factions form. Positions become entrenched. As with many open networks, hierarchies of power emerge and those with the skills, time, resources or sheer stamina can unfairly influence outcomes. The well-documented unrepresentative nature of most open peer networks becomes obvious, and the initial dream of democracy falls by the wayside.

What would it mean for a network to be participatory *and representative*? Are the two words mutually exclusive? Is this another oxymoron? If participants were a randomly selected subset of the entire community, ensuring it mirrored the community from which it was taken, could it still be described as participatory? For those passionate activists dreaming of having their say, perhaps the answer is no. But for those randomly selected, the vast majority of whom would never have participated in a political meeting, then the answer is probably yes. What about everyone else? Would you consider a randomly selected group of people – which included someone your age and gender, with your educational level and from your area – to be a participatory gathering or an exclusive one? Would it make a difference if you knew that you had had an equal chance of being selected?

The key question is one of legitimacy. Perhaps splitting hairs over the meaning of 'participatory' is a distracting side issue. In any case, Part Three will address these topics further.

Notes

1. Charles Leadbeater, 'We are Born to Co-operate', *Guardian Weekly*, 16 March 2012; see also Richard Sennett, *Together: The Rituals, Pleasures and Politics of Cooperation* (Yale University Press, 2012); and Owen Jones, 'Inequality is Not a Human Instinct', *Guardian Weekly*, 28 November 2014.

2. Hardt and Negri, *Commonwealth*, 162.

3. http://radio-weblogs.com/0110772/2002/10/09.html.

4. Shirky, *Everybody*, 20, 159.

5. For example, http://www.crikey.com.au/2013/08/16/newspaper-circulation-results-shocker-the-contagion-edition/; and http://www.iab.net/about_the_iab/recent_press_releases/press_release_archive/press_release/pr-060313.

6. Marc Andreessen, 'Why Software is Eating the World', *Wall Street Journal*, 20 August 2011, see: http://online.wsj.com/news/articles/SB10001424053111903480904576512250915629460.

7. Shirky, *Everybody*, 66.

8. See Barry Ritholtz, 'Smart Investors are Tweeps', *Guardian Weekly*, 26 April 2013, for the effect of Twitter on journalism and investor trading; Unbound.co.uk is a crowd-funding platform for book publishing.

9. Austin Weber, *Outsourcing the Line*, http://www.assemblymag.com/articles/84382-outsourcing-the-line.

10. The open-source operating system, Linux, runs over 90 per cent of mainframes and supercomputers, and although closed-source operating systems dominate the desktop and laptop market (probably around 95–98 per cent), tablets and smartphones present a complicated picture. Android, the most popular mobile phone operating system, is open-source (based on a Linux kernel), and Apple uses a free and open-source operating system (Darwin) underneath many of its most successful products. See, for example, http://en.wikipedia.org/wiki/Web_content_management_system, and http://en.wikipedia.org/wiki/Usage_share_of_operating_systems.

11. There are many examples listed on http://p2pfoundation.net/. For bitcoins and blockchains, see Don Tapscott and Alex Tapscott, *Blockchain Revolution* (Portfolio, 2016), and for the drug reference, see Mike Power, *Drugs*

2.0: The Web Revolution That's Changing How the World Gets High (Portobello, 2013). In mental health, see Mike Slade, 'It Helps if You've Been There', *Guardian Weekly*, 9 March 2012.

12. Michel Bauwens, Nicolas Mendoza and Franco Iacomella, *et al.*, *A Synthetic Overview of the Collaborative Economy*, http://p2p.coop/files/reports/collaborative-economy-2012.pdf; Rachel Botsman and Roo Rogers, *What's Mine Is Yours: The Rise of Collaborative Consumption* (Harper Business, 2010).

13. Cass R. Sunstein, *Infotopia: How Many Minds Produce Knowledge* (Oxford University Press, 2006), 19. This book is surely, at least in part, subject to this problem!

14. John Naughton, 'Our Tools Are Failing Us', *Guardian Weekly*, 16 August 2013.

15. Eli Pariser, 'In Our Own Little Internet Bubbles', *Guardian Weekly*, 26 June 2011.

16. https://www.theguardian.com/environment/2016/apr/17/boaty-mcboatface-wins-poll-to-name-polar-research-vessel.

Chapter 10: The Good, the Bad and the Network

If the economic, technological and cultural shift to the informational, network society is a complex transition holding out positive promises, it also has considerable drawbacks. Melvin Kranzberg's first law of technology captures the idea: technology is neither good nor bad; nor is it neutral.[1]

Structurally, networks can represent the democratic ideal of equality, and the autonomy of nodes in a network is closely related to the concept of open participation. When open standards and protocols structure interaction and communication within a network, then there are few constraints on the composition, both externally and internally, of the individual nodes. Implicit in this is a support for (or at least a healthy disregard of) the diversity of contributors. It is for this reason that imposing homogeneity across a network is unnecessary, beyond agreeing to open standards of communication. The ability to tolerate difference and operate with a multiplicity of node types is often a network's key strength. Not that there is any tolerance for people who vandalise Wikipedia pages, but the process is wilfully oblivious to questions of a participant's gender, race, sexual identity, socio-economic status, geographical location and so forth. Respect for diversity, freedom to participate and the cooperative nature of peer-to-peer processes are all positive characteristics.

Open networks are, however, notoriously unequal in resource distribution and influence, and autonomy does not necessarily imply respect. A glance at any open online forum and the vitriol spilling forth from people's keyboards should be enough to convince anyone that respect is often the first casualty of online autonomy and anonymity.

The participatory nature of networks is also a double-edged sword. Giving voice to disempowered people must be a democratic good. Representative democracy, as it is now practised, patently fails to listen to and adequately incorporate the voices of large segments of the population, and so the attraction of some kind of direct participatory democracy is easy to understand. Unfortunately, it is difficult, if not impossible, to implement since open networks fail profoundly when it comes to representational equality: they do not mirror society. Legal juries are not open and voluntary precisely for this reason – their legitimacy stems from the equal probability of each person being selected.

That networks efficiently and easily lend themselves to the development of processes and the production of immaterial assets is promising. Our laws are precisely this kind of entity. However, the process will be crucial. Throwing a random selection of people into a room and asking them to make laws would most likely fail. It is important to learn from democratic experiments about what works and what does not. The processes must be deliberative, with reason-giving in moral terms paramount.

Political decisions are invariably moral decisions; every question about how to distribute limited resources among competing demands is irrevocably a moral question. So where, if anywhere, does morality lie in a network? This is not a question posed by network theory, but it will be addressed below in Part Three. Pre-empting these arguments, the assumption here is that informed deliberation under respectful conditions can lead to moral outcomes. But are there examples of respectful deliberation in networks?

It would appear difficult, although not impossible, to create open, respectful, deliberative and reason-giving processes online. Wikipedia, again, is perhaps one of the better examples. On every article's separate 'talk' page the decision-making is documented and transparent, and anyone can trace the arguments and process that led to the appearance (or not) of a sentence or idea in an article. Reasons must be given, and can be rejected or countered through appeals to credible sources. It is a kind of deliberation.

Another example is in open-source software programming. Anyone can look at open-source code and try to understand how it accomplishes its task; every significant modification to the code will typically be documented with lists of bugs fixed or features introduced, and its acceptance will depend on this and the resulting discussion. Networked processes can exist that come to reasoned decisions.

There have been several impressive attempts to incorporate deliberation into online decision-making, such as Loomio, Liquid-Feedback and DemocracyOS. Loomio lets users propose, discuss and ideally develop a shared understanding of the issues surrounding a proposal, before justifying the final decision (or vote) to the group. LiquidFeedback and DemocracyOS are somewhat similar to each other, in that they enable members to use transitive, delegated voting whereby a member can give authority to trusted people to vote on their behalf, and limit that delegation to a specific time frame or for specific issues. These are but three of numerous examples of collaborative decision-making software that attempts to incorporate deliberation and reason-giving into online peer-to-peer networks.

In academic experiments, with selective participation, the quality of the deliberation among relatively small online communities has been tracked and analysed.[2] Unsurprisingly, highly structured processes, often among closed communities, typically produce higher-quality deliberation in online political discussions than that experienced in open forums.

It is a matter of ongoing debate among the practitioners and theoreticians of deliberative democracy as to whether these examples of online (text-based) deliberation have approached the standards of deliberation achieved in highly structured, facilitated and face-to-face meetings. Humans, obviously, communicate with more than just words. Facial expressions, body language, tone of voice – all of these give important cues that will affect how people interact face to face. In online forums, however, it has been proposed that 'the lack of physical presence and reduction in social cues [are] useful rather than limiting'. Vincent Price observes that online deliberation:

> ... might actually reduce patterns of social dominance. Studies demonstrate that online discussions are generally much more egalitarian than face-to-face encounters, with reduced patterns of individual dominance and increased contributions by low-status participants... Task-oriented groups generate more unique ideas working in computer-mediated settings than when face-to-face... Group decision-making experiments generally indicate that online discussions, relative to face-to-face group meetings, generate more open exchanges of ideas...[3]

Intuitively, face-to-face assemblies would appear to give the best opportunity for quality deliberation, but we should be open to the possibility that this may not necessarily be so. The results of further studies and experiments will be very interesting, and as technologies such as Skype blur the distinction between online and face-to-face encounters, the results will surely be complicated. Nevertheless, whether democratic deliberation is online, face to face or a hybrid of the two, what is most important is ensuring equality of voice and providing a tolerant and respectful environment where everyone is encouraged to participate meaningfully.

Given that organic and open networks are commonly unrepresentative sites with high levels of inequality, the peer network proposed in Part Three as a replacement for our parliaments is therefore necessarily a highly artificial one. To be legitimate and successful it must be representative and deliberative, and founded on the ideals of equality and respect. These do not occur spontaneously in most participatory networks.

Has the time come for the next revolution in how we do democracy? Perhaps the most important changes are the cultural impacts of technological change, as the quote commonly attributed to Marshall McLuhan runs: 'We shape our tools and thereafter our tools shape us.'[4] Shirky puts it this way:

> Communication tools don't get socially interesting until they get technologically boring... It's when technology becomes normal, then ubiquitous, and finally so pervasive as to be invisible, that the really profound changes happen... Revolution doesn't happen when society adopts new technologies – it happens when society adopts new behaviours... [and often the] social effects lag behind technological ones by decades.[5]

A few decades have already passed. Many of the current generation of adolescents and young adults (at least in the global north) have been bathed in participatory digital communications since birth. There are almost no questions they cannot get a variety of opinions about with a few taps on – or words spoken at – a screen. These social and cultural changes are progressing in unison with the changes outlined above occurring in workplaces, education, politics, research institutions and leisure time. The many positive aspects of these changes are rapidly becoming new norms of modern processes and behaviour: participation, collaboration, transparency and open communication. As Hardt and Negri would have it, network processing 'is not only a model for political decision-making but also tends itself to become political decision-making'.[6]

We can fix our broken politics using the tools, skills and deliberative processes to collaborate and decide on important matters together.

We must, however, be careful. It should be clear by now that there are many pitfalls and risks lurking within peer-to-peer networks. The challenge is to seize upon the positive aspects while being wary of the inherent inequalities and potential difficulties associated with network processes. It will be important to learn together in transparent ways that are respectful of diversity. As will be seen in Part Three, examples already exist whereby networks are constructed to be representative, and deliberative processes can be utilised to incorporate the ideals of equality, participation and mutual respect.

Our laws, governmental policies and societal priorities can be legitimately determined through new participatory mechanisms using processes and skills fast becoming not only commonplace but ubiquitous. Once we realise this, where does it leave our current version of representative democracy? Modern democracy emerged at a time when the telegraph was the best long-distance means of communication, when networks were costly to establish and maintain, and when sending an elected representative to the capital to promote the interests of a constituency seemed like the only option.

This seems no more than a remnant of a past age. We are moving on, and fortunately we have working models of exactly what a real democracy would look like. The communication revolution has made it possible to govern ourselves; the only question is: are we scared of that much freedom?

Notes

1. Melvin Kranzberg, 'Technology and History: "Kranzberg's Laws"', *Technology and Culture*, 1986, Vol. 27, No. 3, 544–60.

2. Todd Davies and Seeta Peña Gangadharan (eds), *Online Deliberation: Design, Research, and Practice* (Center for the Study of Language and Information, 2009).

3. Vincent Price, 'Citizens Deliberating Online: Theory and Some Evidence' in Davies and Gangadharan (eds), *Online Deliberation*, 43.

4. It would appear that the quote is actually a paraphrase by one of his friends; see, for example, http://apennings.com/uncategorized/we-shape-our-tools-and-thereafter-our-tools-shape-us/.

5. Shirky, *Everybody*, 105–6, 159 and 67 respectively.

6. Hardt and Negri, *Multitude*, 336, 339.

Part III: Real Democracy Now

'A real democracy of the rule of all by all based on relationships of equality and freedom... is a dream created in the great revolutions of modernity but never yet realized.'

–Michael Hardt and Antonio Negri

Chapter 11: Empowered Participatory Governance

Since the 1990s, citizens' summits and participatory governance structures involving everyday people have spread across the world and become increasingly common. Politicians and bureaucrats are choosing – or being forced – to open up the process of decision-making whereby 'ordinary citizens... deliberate political issues that are often complex and contentious'.[1] People are deciding together which issues should get priority, how government money should be spent and how best to implement and monitor laws that affect their communities.

In the UK, Anthony King describes 'a sea change in British ideas about nothing less than democracy itself' that germinated in the 'romantic revolt' of the 1960s. Before this time:

> Government was permanent. Democracy was periodic...
> In the years between elections... [there] was no institutional means by which the public at large could impose its will on a government. Government in Britain was not by the people – and almost no one ever suggested that it should be. But ideas about democracy have changed.[2]

Quoting British Prime Minister Clement Attlee in 1945, King illustrates just how dramatically ideas have shifted:

> I could not consent to the introduction into our political life of a device so alien to all our traditions as the referendum, which has only too often been the instrument of Nazism and Fascism.[3]

The first British referendum, on whether the UK should stay in the European Community, was held in 1975. This formed part of the slow acceptance and increasing number of participatory events between elections – within a few decades the involvement of, or at least consultation with, ordinary people about significant political decisions was becoming widespread.

Around the globe, new participatory governance experiments have ranged across the entire variety of governmental levels, from the local to the national and international, and across a broad spectrum of forum size, from fewer than 100 participants up into the thousands. Relatively small-scale examples include municipal participatory budgeting, occurring in 'hundreds or perhaps thousands of locales... from Albania to Zambia' (and many places in between), according to Anwar Shah in a World Bank report.[4] Large-scale events and summits have included the British Columbia Citizens' Assembly on Electoral Reform in Canada in 2004; European Meeting of the Minds in 2005 and Citizens' Consultation in 2007 and 2009; an Australian Citizens' Parliament in 2009; the Icelandic National Gathering on the Constitution in 2010; Belgium's G1000 Citizens' Summit in 2011; and Ireland's 'We the Citizens' National Citizens' Assembly in 2011, its Constitutional Convention from 2012–14 and another citizens' assembly that began in October 2016.[5] In the run-up to Chile's general election in 2013, several presidential candidates proposed a citizens' assembly to rewrite the country's constitution.[6] Some of the above summits (Ireland's convention and second assembly, and the ones in British Columbia and Iceland) were mandated by the state; others operated outside state structures (Ireland's first assembly, and those in Australia and Belgium) and attempted to influence government decisions through publicity and the sheer weight of numbers and diversity of the people involved. Most of these assemblies relied on the legitimacy inherent in using, at least in part, a randomly selected representative sample of people with an informed, deliberative process.

Modern participatory budgeting began in Porto Alegre, Brazil, in 1989; it allows citizens to participate in the planning, funding, delivery and monitoring of the provision of public goods and services. Though 'very different types and levels of citizen engagement with public resource decisions and service delivery are referred to as participatory budgeting', their common element is a variety of assemblies where people decide how to allocate a (generally small) portion of the municipal budget to local projects that affect them directly, and whose implementation they can easily observe and follow.[7] When the participation is meaningful, it will typically increase the accountability, transparency and effectiveness of government spending by aligning it more closely with the needs of the citizens it is supposed to serve. The levels of participation can be impressive: in one year alone in Porto Alegre over 20,000 citizens are estimated to have been involved, and 8.4 per cent of the adult population stated they had participated in the previous five years.[8] The idea has spread to the US and to several cities in Europe: in Paris in 2014 the largest sum ever, 426 million euros, was allocated to a single participatory budgeting process.

Citizens' assemblies, deliberative polls and citizens' or policy juries differ from participatory budgeting. In these forums, often the participants are randomly selected, and, as a consequence, the group can aim for descriptive representation of the relevant population, which ensures a diversity of voices and opinions. Other events of a somewhat similar nature, such as planning cells in Germany and consensus conferences in Denmark, often use different selection methods, as detailed by Graham Smith in *Democratic Innovations*.[9] Here, the focus is restricted to those forums that, unlike an open public meeting or self-selected or 'stakeholder' group, do use random selection to choose participants from the relevant constituency.

The Icelandic Constitutional Act specified that people be randomly sampled from the National Population Register for the National Gathering on the Constitution – 950 people eventually participated – to voice 'the principal viewpoints and points of emphasis of the public concerning the organisation of the country's government and its constitution'.[10] The provincial government of British Columbia, Canada, created the Citizens' Assembly on Electoral Reform, in which 158 randomly selected members (one male and one female from each constituency) met throughout 2004 to develop an electoral reform proposal that was put to a referendum.[11] Ireland's Constitutional Convention, mandated by the government, randomly selected two-thirds of its participants – reserving the remaining third for politicians – to review a set of constitutional issues and topics. One outcome of the convention was the proposal that resulted in the successful referendum on legalising same-sex marriage in Ireland in 2015. The Australian Citizens' Parliament in 2009 and Belgium's G1000 Citizens' Summit were organised by research and civil society groups. The former randomly selected 150 participants to deliberate on the question, 'How can Australia's political system be strengthened to serve us better?'; the latter managed to attract 704 people to discuss a variety of contentious political questions and issues in Belgium after a record period of national political stalemate. Several Europe-wide events have also been held: the Meeting of the Minds in 2005 randomly selected panels of 14 citizens in nine European countries to deliberate on the ethics of brain science and related EU policy.[12] European Citizens' Consultations organised in 2006–7 and 2009 also randomly selected a representative sample of citizens and combined national panels and pan-European deliberation (typically in Brussels) to formulate recommendations about a variety of social and economic issues.

Descriptive representation is often the aim of such forums. To obtain a more accurate reflection of the community at large, and to not, for example, over-represent older, better-educated men, the random selection is often *stratified*: once the number of men in the sample reaches 50 per cent of the total, no more men are invited to participate. The same idea can be applied to age brackets, income, location, education level and so forth. The random selection *increases* the perceived legitimacy of such forums, as it avoids any potential takeover by well-organised special interests or political lobbies, and the process of stratification avoids a common problem of self-selection to open meetings, whereby a forum 'disproportionately attracts politically active, highly educated, high income and older participants'.[13]

Of these types of forums, policy juries are typically smaller than deliberative polls, which are usually smaller than citizens' assemblies. The aim, though, is broadly the same: to inform a representative sample of citizens on certain issues and facilitate deliberation leading to an understanding of the relative popularity of specific policy options. It is emphatically neither a raw opinion poll nor a referendum. Deliberation informed by balanced and accurate information is a key element: the outcome should measure not what people in general *do* think, but what they *would* think, given the time, information and possibility to argue their point of view and be affected by the views of others in a facilitated and fair setting. As Lyn Carson says, deliberation moves beyond public *opinion* to public *judgement*.[14] Dryzek calls this the 'simulation claim' – that a mini-public should give 'a simulation of what the population as a whole would decide if everyone were allowed to deliberate'.[15]

In Denmark and Germany, planning cells have been used since the 1970s, and the Jefferson Center in the US has been promoting deliberative forums since the same time, primarily in Minnesota. In the UK it has been estimated that there were 'at least five hundred [citizen jury]-type exercises between 1996 and 2006'.[16] Denmark's Board of Technology has expanded from planning cells to coordinating global days of deliberation, such as the World Wide Views on Climate and Energy event in 2015, involving approximately 10,000 participants from almost 100 countries spanning six continents.[17] In Australia in 2014, a randomly selected 'Melbourne People's Panel' developed a ten-year, AU$4 billion financial plan for the City of Melbourne – and this is but one example of many such forums organised by the newDemocracy Foundation in that country.[18]

Deliberative Polling® is the technique developed in 1988 by James Fishkin of Stanford University, whereby participants' opinions are compared before and after engaging in informed deliberation with other citizens.[19] These deliberative polls have been held on many different topics across the globe, from crime to energy policy to indigenous reconciliation. Another example is the EuroPolis project in 2009 in Brussels, where 348 participants from all the EU-member states at the time were randomly selected and deliberated on climate change and immigration policy (with real-time translation), directing questions to panels of politicians and experts. The result was a distinct shift by many attendees towards more progressive views on both topics after the event: 'Before deliberation 49% wanted to maximize combating climate change. After deliberation this rose to 61%... [T]hose who thought that "immigration increases crime in our society" fell from 48% to 40%.'[20]

When the number of randomly selected citizens deliberating at a gathering is in the hundreds (as opposed to policy juries with perhaps 20 or 30 attendees), it is easier to assume that it will be a more representative sample of the diversity of a community, lending the process even greater legitimacy. Larger assemblies, however, will be logistically more difficult to organise, and more expensive. In Melbourne in 2007, an inner-city municipality brought a randomly selected, representative sample of 750 people together to successfully deliberate on, and prioritise items for, a ten-year community plan. The one-day gathering cost AU$230,000, excluding council staff time.[21]

Although one goal of stratified random selection is to ensure that an assembly 'looks like' the community it is taken from, the larger goal is to make better policy by incorporating a representative sample of the diversity of desires and viewpoints present within society into the deliberative process, and ultimately into any final decisions.

It could, however, be argued that there is no proof that the diversity of *viewpoints* in society necessarily follows demographic or socio-economic lines.[22] Perhaps the random selection should be stratified according to how many people share a specific viewpoint? Some diversity of perspectives, however, surely does follow socio-economic and demographic lines, and in the absence of widely accepted ways to measure and group viewpoints and perspectives, selecting *large* numbers of people from across the demographic and socio-economic spectrum is the best way to approach the goal.

Another common concern is that as participation in events such as citizens' juries is voluntary, and there is typically a very low response rate to invitations – five per cent is considered impressive – the selection will never reflect the broader populace perfectly. There will always be, in voluntary events, some inevitable element of self-selection and bias among those who respond to the initial invitation: in the British Columbia citizens' assembly 'participants tended to be more politically knowledgeable and civically active than the general population'.[23] As such, the process should be more accurately described as near-random, or quasi-random selection. Indeed, it is often difficult for these forums to attract participants who are young, of low income or from disadvantaged minorities, and more direct forms of outreach are sometimes employed to reach these people. At the G1000 in Belgium, 10 per cent of the assembly seats were reserved for people from disadvantaged groups, who were approached directly through trusted civil society organisations and charities.

In any case, the self-selection bias when using stratified random sampling can often be greatly reduced, through monetary incentives and individual, tailored support to assist participation. When compared to the heavily skewed attendance at open forums, random sampling leads to significantly higher levels of diversity – direct invitation *does* bring in people who would not usually attend a political meeting, and stratification by age, gender and educational attainment can achieve a good approximation of descriptive representation.

Ultimately, the aim of such forums is not *perfect* legitimacy (whatever that may mean) but *increased* legitimacy. The goal is better, not perfect, representation. These are not stakeholder meetings, or meetings stacked with partisan campaigners or the disgruntled, nor are they full of politicians with one eye on the media, the polls and the next election campaign. If one compares how descriptively representative these forums are to how descriptively representative our parliaments are, it is clear which is closer to the general population. They are forums that attempt to mirror the community from which they are drawn, and are therefore often referred to as mini-publics. The demographic and socio-economic stratification also has a conceptual simplicity that is easy to communicate, and the resulting descriptively representative assembly is intuitively appealing, both of which are important benefits.

It is the use of random selection and deliberation that differentiates citizens' assemblies from processes such as participatory budgeting. Below, it will be argued that it is random selection, as opposed to self-selection or competitive election, that distinguishes these events as especially democratic, and is crucial to their legitimacy. An assembly that uses random selection, and facilitated deliberation, will more closely simulate the public judgements of the general populace than our parliaments currently do.

Historically, random selection was seen as the *sine qua non* of democracy, at least until the expansion of voting rights led to constitutional government being rechristened as democratic government. The recent rediscovery that random selection has an implicit legitimacy forms the basis for the proposition, outlined below, that random selection of decision-makers (or sortition) is a viable, balanced and less corruptible method for populating our legislative assemblies. It will be argued that a government formed using sortition would be legitimate, accountable, competent and efficient; the laws it would amend and develop, covering the full range of complex and contentious topics confronting society, would reflect a representative sample of people's informed views. It would be a group of peers, producing laws, and it should be structured like a network.

Democracy cannot, and never should, be reduced to the activities of a handful of local or national assemblies. Democracy is a process that must, if it is to prosper, involve many institutions, groups and individuals interacting in highly complex ways. Dryzek argues that focusing only on individual institutions severely limits the deliberative democratic agenda: 'a mini-public in and of itself never can and never should be mistaken for a deliberative democracy'.[24] Many other deliberative democracy academics also believe that 'no single forum, however ideally constituted, could possess deliberative capacity sufficient to legitimate most of the decisions and policies that democracies adopt'.[25] Democracy is, in short, a system.[26] Which explains why leaders with authoritarian tendencies, from Turkey to Russia to China and many other places, suppress or severely constrain the media and civil society. A free media, active civil society, independent judiciary, the protection of various rights of assembly and protest, and limitations on the powers of any legislature are crucial to any functioning democracy. Democracy is much more than its legislatures, and far more than the mode of appointment to its legislatures, so a deliberative democracy would be much more than a deliberative legislature. A deliberative *system* would involve all the interacting components of society. While this book focuses on the institutions of parliament and congress, it does not dismiss the importance of enhancing deliberation between and across other institutions within society. Nevertheless, given the many caveats mentioned above, most deliberative democracy academics applaud and encourage the spread of individual deliberative institutions and experiments.

The focus on legislatures in this book is not intended to detract from these other important modes of participation and societal deliberation, which should not be neglected in any democracy. Many different techniques and processes of public engagement and participation are needed to make governments more responsive to citizens, to keep decision-makers accountable, and to build the necessary trust and capacity among people and bureaucrats to interact with each other respectfully. Many impressive examples of citizen participation are documented in the OECD's *Focus on Citizens: Public Engagement for Better Policy and Services*.[27] Further examples are detailed on the website www.participedia.net, and in an extensive range of academic papers and civil society publications and books, such as *The Deliberative Democracy Handbook*.[28] The general picture in the latter book is of people willingly engaging in deliberative forums discussing complex and contentious issues, mostly enjoying the experience, regularly changing their view as a result of the process, and often surprising and impressing experts with their understanding and decisions.[29] There are still many obstacles to genuine inclusivity in randomly selected groups (for example, in US juries men typically talk more than women[30]) and quality deliberation – and even debate about how to define and measure the quality of deliberation – but strategies are emerging to manage, and at least partially mitigate, these problems. As Amy Gutmann and Dennis Thompson state:

> There is certainly a broad scope for reasonable disagreement about how much deliberation is sufficient, whether a particular instance of deliberation is as good as it can be, and whether the ensuing decision is just. But 'sufficient,' 'as good as it can be,' and 'just' are ideal standards, and failing to meet them does not render a deliberative decision illegitimate.[31]

Across the wide variety of participatory forums, it is important to distinguish clearly between community *empowerment* and community *engagement*. The degree of empowerment – whether the decisions are binding on governments or the relevant agencies, or if they will be put to referenda, or are merely advice or suggestions – varies significantly across all the examples above. Alta Fölscher differentiates 'two broad types of citizen engagement, distinguished by the degree to which citizens enter the action space of the state'.[32] Lobbying, and direct democratic control, are posited as the lower and upper extremes on this ladder of participation. There is justified criticism of much of the use of citizens' juries as tokenistic and the democratic equivalent of whitewash, whereby a government can claim a higher degree of legitimacy by pointing to the existence of an exercise that, if done poorly, bears more resemblance to a focus group run by an advertising agency. In *Democratic Innovations*, Smith mentions the 'common criticism' that many participatory exercises have 'little or no effect on decisions' and are prone to 'the suspicion that participation has at best little effect on the decision-making process and at worst is no more than a mode of manipulation and co-optation by political elites to legitimise decisions made elsewhere'.[33] The aim must always be empowerment, not mere engagement.

An empowered participatory democracy would involve not only legitimising processes, adequate time and highly trained, unbiased facilitators and experts, but its outcomes would be guaranteed at the outset to be adopted by the relevant government or authority. Similar to Fölscher and the work cited therein by McGee, the International Association for Public Participation outlines a spectrum of involvement that also has empowered decision-making at the highest end of increasing levels of public impact.[34]

The model of empowered participatory governance outlined in *Deepening Democracy*, edited by Archon Fung and Erik Olin Wright, focuses on ordinary people solving tangible and specific problems through deliberation.[35] The unique institutional feature they identify that stabilises the practice is 'coordinated decentralisation', where 'the learning capacity of the system as a whole... may be enhanced by the combination of decentralised empowered deliberation and centralised coordination and feedback'. It is a network structure where the maintenance of open channels of communication and the diffusion of information and expertise, but no decision-making power, are the responsibility of a coordinating secretariat. These peer networks can collectively produce and improve processes that are invariably owned by everyone in the network. These normative principles are then used to assess the performance of several participatory case studies from various areas, including infrastructure, schooling, policing and environmental policy. Departures from ideal practice, such as deliberation degenerating into conflict or inactivity, and the lack of capacities for effective participation, are recognised, along with attempts to alleviate the problems through training or direct intervention. Indeed, the general problem when deliberation is done by self-selecting partici-pants is that the 'rule of the reasoners (not of reason) is likely to com-pound existing social inequalities. According to some critics, we can expect a preponderance of the economically advantaged, or men, or those otherwise possessed of cultural capital and argumentative confi-dence.'[36] This issue is surely recognised by all who have attended an open, public forum – and is precisely what random selection can help avoid.

The broad sweep of arenas and processes where citizens' voices are sought in government decision-making supports the claim made in the OECD's *Focus on Citizens* that: 'We are currently living through an interesting period of intense [democratic] experimenta-tion as we strive to create new solutions, fit for the citizens of the new millennium.'[37] Even given the imperfect nature of many forays into participatory practices, calls for *less* participation by citizens in the development of governmental policy are today rarely heard.

Notes

1. Dryzek with Niemeyer, *Foundations*, 155.

2. King, *Britain*, 114–15.

3. King, *Britain*, 16.

4. Anwar Shah (ed.), *Participatory Budgeting* (The International Bank for Reconstruction and Development/The World Bank, 2007), 5–6. According to The Worldwatch Institute's *State of the World 2007: Our Urban Future* (W. W. Norton & Company, 2007), 180–1: 'Between 2000 and 2006, the total number of cities with participatory budgets grew from 200 to roughly 1,200.'

5. http://www.participedia.net/en/cases/icelandic-national-forum-2010; http://g1000.org/en; http://www.wethecitizens.ie/; and see still more examples here: http://www.parliament.uk/documents/commons/lib/research/briefings/snpc-04482.pdf.

6. Jonathon Franklin, 'Battle Lines Set as Protestors Press for an Overhaul of Chile's Political System', *Guardian Weekly*, 5 July 2013.

7. Alta Fölscher, 'Participatory Budgeting in Asia', in Shah (ed.), *Participatory Budgeting*, 244, 246. See also Shah, *Participatory Budgeting*, 45.

8. Quoted on http://www.participedia.net/en/cases/participatory-budgeting-porto-alegre. See also Graham Smith, *Democratic Innovations* (Cambridge University Press, 2009), Chapter Two.

9. Smith, *Innovations*, 77.

10. http://www.participedia.net/en/cases/icelandic-national-forum-2010.

11. Although 95 per cent of the participants supported the final referendum proposal, and it achieved a 58 per cent approval rating at the referendum, the legislation stipulated that a vote of 60 per cent would be required to change the electoral laws, and therefore no change was made.

12. http://www.brainscienceeurope.org/; https://www.ceps.eu/system/files/book/1856.pdf; http://participedia.net/en/cases/european-citizens-consultation-2009.

13. Dryzek with Niemeyer, *Foundations*, 156.

14. See, for example, Lyn Carson, https://griffithreview.com/articles/dilemmas-disasters-and-deliberative-democracy/.

15. Dryzek with Niemeyer, *Foundations*, 27.

16. Peter Reason and Hilary Bradbury (eds), *Handbook of Action Research*, second edition (Sage Inc., 2007), 336. See also http://www.parliament.uk/documents/commons/lib/research/briefings/snpc-04546.pdf.

17. See http://climateandenergy.wwviews.org; and a prior event in 2009: http://globalwarming.wwviews.org.

18. http://participate.melbourne.vic.gov.au/10yearplan.

19. James Fishkin, *When the People Speak: Deliberative Democracy and Public Consultation* (Oxford University Press, 2011).

20. See http://www.circap.org/uploads/1/8/1/6/18163511/eu09executivesummary.pdf. See also a similar event, Tomorrow's Europe, held in 2007: http://cdd.stanford.edu/polls/eu/2007/eu-dpoll-pressrelease.pdf.

21. OECD, *Focus on Citizens*, 85.

22. The link between cognitive (or discourse) diversity and socio-economic diversity is not necessarily straightforward, and is explored both in Scott E. Page, *The Difference: How the Power of Diversity Creates Better Groups, Firms, Schools and Societies* (Princeton University Press, 2007), 13, 14, 299, 325; and Dryzek with Niemeyer, *Foundations*, 35–41.

23. Smith, *Innovations*, 81. See also 80–3 for more on this topic.

24. Dryzek with Niemeyer, *Foundations*, 176.

25. John Parkinson and Jane Mansbridge (eds), *Deliberative Systems: Deliberative Democracy at the Large Scale* (Cambridge University Press, 2012), 1.

26. John Parkinson and Jane Mansbridge (eds), *Deliberative Systems: Deliberative Democracy at the Large Scale* (Cambridge University Press, 2012), 1.

27. OECD, *Focus on Citizens*.

28. For example, http://www.involve.org.uk/wp-content/uploads/2013/02/From-Fairy-Tale-to-Reality.pdf; John Gastil and Peter Levine (eds), *The Deliberative Democracy Handbook: Strategies for Effective Civic Engagement in the 21st Century* (Jossey-Bass, 2005). This paragraph in effect summarises 272–3.

29. A prominent dissenter from the rosy picture of deliberation painted here is Sunstein, *Infotopia*, 12, 55–7, 70, 184; he argues, repeatedly referring to the same three examples, that deliberation can polarise attendees, or sometimes lead to 'groupthink'. The relevance of his findings to randomly selected deliberative forums is questioned in Dryzek with Niemeyer, *Foundations*, 161. Sunstein's claim that decisions can be 'correct' or 'accurate' also presupposes a mythical best outcome from deliberation; most interesting political questions are the result of

complex situations and legitimate alternate policy decisions will exist depending on priorities.

30. Gastil and Levine, *Deliberative Democracy*, 279.

31. Amy Gutmann and Dennis Thompson, *Why Deliberative Democracy?* (Princeton University Press, 2004), 179.

32. Fölscher, 'Participatory', in Shah (ed.), *Participatory Budgeting*, 246–7.

33. Smith, *Innovations*, 23, 169; see also 18.

34. http://www.iap2.org/associations/4748/files/IAP2 Spectrum_vertical.pdf.

35. Archon Fung and Erik Olin Wright (eds), *Deepening Democracy: Institutional Innovations in Empowered Participatory Governance* (Verso, 2002). Quote below is from 25.

36. Fung and Wright, *Deepening*, 245.

37. OECD, *Focus on Citizens*, 300.

Chapter 12: Sortition: An Old Idea for New Times

If imitation is the sincerest form of flattery, one particular style of participatory meeting, Fishkin's Deliberative Polling, is very widely respected.

These meetings randomly select participants, who are often assembled at tables of eight to ten people, accompanied by a trained, neutral facilitator, with the deliberation alternating between plenary presentations and small-table discussions. They deliberate about and respond to proposals of 'collective political will or public judgement', and have been held on an impressively wide array of topics, from crime and healthcare to economic policy, political reform and more.[1] Encouraging interaction between diverse people is of prime importance. The participants are paid, and polled both at the start and the end of the event, so that changes in opinion due to the deliberation can be assessed. According to Sean Gray: 'Almost every Deliberative Polling experiment conducted thus far has also resulted in a number of large and statistically significant changes of opinion.'[2]

The now defunct not-for-profit organisation AmericaSpeaks used a similar process in its 21st Century Town Meetings. These meetings were used by local, state and national bodies, most famously in the Listening to the City summit (with 4,500 participants) to discuss the redevelopment of Lower Manhattan after the 11 September 2001 terrorist attacks, and in 2006 when its Unified New Orleans Plan community congresses prioritised redevelopment projects in the wake of Hurricane Katrina. In 2010, it engaged 3,500 people in Our Budget, Our Economy meetings across the country to learn and deliberate on the fiscal issues resulting from the financial crisis and recession of the preceding years. After the deliberative events, high levels of support were expressed from across the country for proposals to reduce defence spending, to 'abandon the failed politics of partisanship' and to give citizen input the same level of importance as is given to powerful lobbying groups.[3]

What is striking to the observer of Deliberative Polling events and 21st Century Town Meetings is the very obvious network structure of the meetings, which have an equally obvious imposed equality.

Each table (or node) is treated equally, and the small group parallel discussions enable everyone to contribute to the outcome efficiently.

In the AmericaSpeaks assemblies, networked computers on each table documented the discussion, allowing common agreements and themes to emerge and be identified and presented to the entire assembly. This highly artificial, imposed network form, where no table is allowed more (or fewer) resources than the others, should not be overlooked. From our understanding of networks above, these elements of process and structure are crucial to the success of these meetings.

The facilitated assemblies organised by AmericaSpeaks, while not the only tool it used, were by far the most eye-catching. Participants, however, were not chosen using random selection. Demographic targets were set, taken from sources such as census data, and outreach strategies were adjusted over time so that the participants would be as close to a demographically and socio-economically representative sample of the population as was feasible. Fishkin is dismissive of this approach, suggesting that it is little better than an open forum, yet without the relevant participant data it is difficult to judge accurately.[4] In any case, many unique elements of the AmericaSpeaks process were designed to overcome shortcomings of the more traditional open consultative assembly.

A 21st Century Town Meeting was not simply an open town hall meeting – AmericaSpeaks did work hard to ensure that the attendees reflected the population from which they were drawn: the aim was for half the people to be women and half men, with proportionate involvement of young and old, the highly educated and the less educated. The participants were dispersed throughout the room and made not only to vote but to deliberate face to face with people from diverse walks of life whom they may have never usually encountered. It was not enough to state an opinion or preference; justifications were sought in terms that the other participants at a table found relevant and not self-serving. These were not your usual community meetings attended only by the disgruntled, the disruptive or the self-interested. And having small-table deliberation meant that strong personalities could not dominate the assembly: trained facilitators tried to make sure they did not even dominate a single table, and that everyone was given an equal opportunity to contribute. Anonymous voting using individual keypads provided the opportunity to quickly and easily conduct straw polls and to prioritise options flowing in from the pool of collective information. Typically, the events were held for one day on a weekend (although preparatory or follow-up events or online discussions could begin before or continue afterwards), and although occasionally the attendees' travel expenses were covered, the time spent at the forum was given voluntarily (unlike in a deliberative poll where attendees are paid). Similar to a deliberative poll, balanced, expert information could be presented easily to the entire assembly for critical inclusion in the discussions, and these experts could be called to individual tables if more clarification was desired.

If random selection had been used to populate the AmericaSpeaks assemblies, they would certainly have represented an impressive embodiment of the positive elements of the deliberative, peer-to-peer networks described in Part Two. As mentioned above, each node (or table) at a 21st Century Town Meeting had an enforced equality – none of them had more influence than any other, and trained facilitators promoted and enforced equality among participants at each table. If sortition had been used, the assembly would have been participatory *by proxy* in the sense that every person from a community could have been asked to attend, but it would not have been open participation, which usually leads directly to bias. Furthermore, stratification could have ensured that the participation was representative and diverse.

When assemblies are organised along these lines, respectful deliberation stems not only from the presence of a facilitator, but is often explicitly agreed to by all involved at the outset, and is anyhow common in such structured, face-to-face environments. The overall process is one of coordinated decentralisation: each table deliberates on a certain topic or issue, initially independently of the other tables, but the network of results is then fed back to the group at large, who can engage in further rounds of deliberation and prioritisation. The immaterial results of this peer network process – the priorities and decisions – are impossible to attribute to any single node: they are owned by all the participants, and one feature commonly reported by attendees at such assemblies is their strong sense of ownership, inclusion and feeling of empowerment.

Although the AmericaSpeaks meetings did not use random selection, it would be relatively easy to do so, as the G1000 in Belgium did (using random telephone dialling) to recruit the vast majority of attendees. Interestingly, the G1000 did not use networked computers on each table (presumably due to cost), but had 'runners' transferring summaries of table discussions and responses to a team of people who amalgamated the results before presenting them to the entire assembly. The agenda of the Belgian G1000 was set by an open, online participatory process, and the top items included topics such as immigration and inequality. After the assembly, a smaller group of volunteers was selected to further develop the assembly's most popular ideas into concrete policy proposals.

In 2014, a few years after the G1000 in Belgium, the first Dutch G1000 took place. Some residents of the city of Amersfoort, with local government support, sent invitations to several thousand randomly selected Amersfoort people. The respondents were brought together with a selection of politicians, civil servants, employers and 'free thinkers' to discuss local priorities and create concrete proposals for the city. The co-founders of the Dutch G1000, Harm van Dijk and Jerphaas Donner, characterised the event as a 'cultural dialogue... a community-building instrument... not [a] participation instrument'.[5] From the outset, the Dutch G1000 was conceived of as 'a new form of relating to each other', a different way of seeking common ground and agreement across the 'whole system' of society – in contrast to the usual confrontational politics. The co-founders see the events as a way of understanding community *needs* and talk of dialogue, not debate – they explicitly request that people put aside disagreement and do not try to convince other participants but, rather, seek common ground. They are confident that, even though such a small percentage of residents are involved in these events (typically less than 1 per cent), the events will have a ripple effect throughout the communities where a G1000 is held regularly.

Unusually, van Dijk and Donner do not see any benefit from facilitation or expert advice. The Amersfoort G1000 began with a blank slate, which guaranteed the independence of the process, but made the inclusion of balanced, expert opinion impossible. In van Dijk and Donner's experience, when experts participate in the process they rapidly constrain or shut down discussion. They similarly believe that having designated table facilitators can interfere and bias group dynamics. A secretary is allocated to each table, but his or her function is strictly to record and clarify, never to contribute or direct discussions. More will be said about reducing the influence of experts and facilitators – and their necessity in many contexts – in the next chapter.

Reserving seats for specific categories of people is relatively common across many of these examples. At the Belgian G1000, 10 per cent of seats were allocated to disadvantaged minorities. In the 2001 deliberative poll on reconciliation with Australia's indigenous population, there was an oversampling of indigenous people. At Ireland's Constitutional Convention, one-third of the seats were reserved for a representative group of politicians. The Dutch G1000s reserve up to 30 per cent of the seats for a range of societal actors, including the privileged, such as employers and politicians, and the hard to reach, such as youths and ethnic minorities. If the aim is descriptive representation, then oversampling underprivileged, hard-to-attract groups is probably a necessity. Politicians are often included in the hope that their inclusion will convince them to take the outcomes seriously: Claudia Chwalisz posits that 'by involving them in the [Irish Constitutional Convention] process, it was ensured that politicians would not feel so alienated as to simply ignore or discard proposals'.[6] However, the second Irish government-mandated assembly, unlike the first, has no seats reserved for politicians (and is underway at the time of this book's publication). In the UK in 2015, two pilot citizens' assemblies were held – one with politicians and one without – to explore the effect of their presence. Although the final report noted that 'we find that in terms of both domination and influence politicians tend to be nominated [by participants as dominant]' the actual numbers involved were too small to be overly significant.[7]

The use of random selection is once again coming to be seen as a tool with which to increase the legitimacy of political forums. The conceptual simplicity of a random, representative and networked selection of everyday people participating in small-table, facilitated deliberation, and deciding on complex and important issues, makes it easy to understand why the model has been so widely imitated. Having informed deliberation mitigates at least a few prejudices, and the people involved have not been lobbied and do not have to follow a party line. They do not have to please financial donors, or keep one eye on the next election and their approval ratings, or worry about creating the perfect media soundbite. All this is closer to what democracy should be able to achieve: deliberation that gets to the crux of the 'legitimate moral differences' that inevitably exist in a free, pluralistic society, and decision-making that flows from this enhanced appreciation.[8] This approaches the democratic ideal of people taking a longer-term, considered and broad view of the public good, rather than what occurs in the current, often polarised political landscape, where inequalities in power dictate the outcomes of a decision-making process determined largely through political bargaining – Dahl's 'dark side' of representative government: the 'nondemocratic... *bargaining among political and bureaucratic elites*.'[9]

As Gutmann and Thompson point out in *Why Deliberative Democracy?*:

... a general defence of bargaining is not likely to be plausible. The main problem with bargaining as a general substitute for deliberation is that it accepts the current distribution of resources and power as a baseline, the place to begin the negotiations. On the face of it, this is not the best site for a moral defence of democratic procedures or outcomes.[10]

Dahl also, many years ago, imagined mini-publics 'of perhaps a thousand citizens randomly selected out of the entire demos' to act in a governmental advisory manner.[11] Advice is, however, easy to ignore, although Healthy Democracy Oregon shows that this is not always the case. They randomly select people to review citizens' proposals that will later be put to referenda. The informed, unbiased and considered opinion of the randomly selected group is distributed to voters and has led, among other things, to a significant decline in the number of spurious proposals; it is also claimed that half of voters consider the citizens' informed opinions when making their own decision. The idea has since spread from Oregon to Arizona and Colorado.

One common criticism of many of the above examples is that they are not empowered and are therefore potentially a waste of time, energy and resources. Many observers, if there is no direct policy outcome that can be measured, or a law that has changed as a result, dismiss deliberative events as little more than interesting experiments. This represents a very narrow view of what success in the political sphere entails. In any case, such a criticism is irrelevant here, as the proposal below is for the *empowered* use of sortition in citizens' assemblies.

Important indirect effects of the examples above should not be ignored. The Dutch co-founders of the G1000 report a significant change in the language and policies of local politicians. The Belgian G1000 had little directly observable impact on Belgian politics, but inspired the Dutch G1000, whose founders insist that the community strengthening effect is paramount. The 'unsuccessful' Australian Citizens' Parliament has led to the newDemocracy Foundation being contracted to facilitate empowered assemblies using sortition across Australia. They have organised over a dozen smaller, randomly selected policy juries to review council budgets, discuss infrastructure and energy questions, or deliberate on public safety, among other topics. Before agreeing to organise any forum, the newDemocracy Foundation now seeks a guarantee from the relevant government body to implement, or at least table for a free debate, the proposed outcomes. The newDemocracy Foundation organises empowered assemblies, not merely consultation or opinion-gathering exercises.

Many other groups and people have also proposed or used random selection in modern times – it is certainly not a new idea. In *Democratic Innovations*, Smith lists several detailed proposals for instituting randomly selected, empowered legislative assemblies, spanning the previous 30 years.[12]

In large, randomly selected assemblies we should expect, as detailed in Chapter Eight, that the network process involved will be highly significant. Almost more important than the *what* is the *how*. From this standpoint, the precise details of structure and the modes of interaction are very important: random selection must be combined with quality deliberation at networked tables for an assembly to enforce equality and diversity of voice and to facilitate the production of common outcomes. The structure and process are important parts of what gives these assemblies their legitimacy.

Deliberative democracy is the political theory that tries to differentiate informed, reasoned decision-making from the usual practice of political horse-trading, or outcomes determined by simple vote-aggregation such as referenda. Gutmann and Thompson define deliberative democracy:

> … as a form of government in which free and equal citizens… justify decisions in a process in which they give one another reasons that are mutually acceptable and generally accessible, with the aim of reaching conclusions that are binding in the present on all citizens but open to challenge in the future.

The key element is 'the need to justify decisions', with reasons that 'should be accepted by free and equal persons seeking fair terms of cooperation'. The reason-giving process of deliberative democracy that 'is necessary for declaring a law to be not only legitimate but also just' implicitly holds that 'persons should be treated not merely as objects of legislation or as passive subjects to be ruled. They should be treated as political agents who take part in governance.'[13]

The Deliberative Polling of Fishkin and the 21st Century Town Meetings of AmericaSpeaks are some of the most impressive embodiments of such deliberative forums to date. The organisers would surely agree with Gutmann and Thompson, who state:

> The underlying assumption is that we should value reaching conclusions through reason rather than force, and more specifically through moral reasoning rather than through self-interested bargaining. Citizens and officials, we assume, can learn how to take each other seriously as moral agents. They can enter the discussion in the political forum with the purpose of discovering principles on which the society as a whole can act, rather than with the aim of devising arguments by which they can advance only their own interest.[14]

The theory of deliberative democracy and the various contemporary practical examples of its implementation provide the inspiration for what a real democracy would look like and how it would function: parliaments should be constituted from a large, randomly selected and representative sample of citizens engaged in facilitated and networked small-table deliberation in an assembly informed by experts. In this setting, they would create, deliberate on and amend laws. The leap in imagination to get to this point is much larger than the leap in practicalities. The electoral process would be replaced by a lottery, and the confrontational design and layout of our legislative assemblies would be extensively renovated to become places suited to intense, informed and networked deliberation.

These representatives – a representative sample of the people – could have fixed parliamentary terms (for example, five years, with a fifth of them being replaced every year) and be paid a certain multiple (say, five) of the median wage so as to make it not only an attractive option to a continuing career, but also a positively lucrative five-year experience for the vast majority of people. Parents with dependants and those performing unpaid care work would need extra support, and systems would need to be in place to deal with the usual workplace issues such as illness, pregnancy, retirement and the like. With sortition, the public would, perhaps, even begin to see something of themselves in the people making and changing the laws, and maybe not despise them so much.[15]

The rest of the system could initially remain untouched: the new representatives would continue to come from every corner of the country to travel to the capital to introduce, deliberate, develop and vote on legislation. They would still have staff to organise engagements with their geographical constituents, and explain and justify their motivations and reasoning to the media. There would still be lawyers employed to flesh out the precise details of the laws, under the government's direction. No doubt the full array of lobbyists and civil society groups would continue to try to attract the representatives' attention and push pet issues up the political agenda, or keep some of them off the agenda altogether. The media would still hound the representatives and demand justifications for decisions. However, powerful vested interests could not threaten to withdraw financial support, or run damaging pre-election media campaigns if they were ignored; none of the new parliamentarians would need to seek corporate (or other) donations, or satisfy the partisan demands of party activists, or go through an expensive, time-consuming election or worry overly much about their media profile.

It is an understatement to say this would represent a radical break with our existing representative democracy. Yet in an interesting historical twist, random selection was how the ancient Greek democracies populated their legislation-drafting bodies, their courts and most of their bureaucracies (and even priests, apparently).[16] After over 2,000 years our modern democratic deficiencies could be attenuated by recalling the democratic style of Athens, updating it for a world where slavery is outlawed and gender equality is paramount, and harnessing the deliberative skills, capacities and network technologies of the modern era. This, then, will be Democracy 2.0.

The political appeal of sortition was so obvious, to ancient Greek men at least, that it was by far their most commonly used process for allocating political posts. As quoted above, Aristotle's statement in *Politics* – 'It is thought to be democratic for the offices [of constitutional government] to be assigned by lot, for them to be elected oligarchic' – would seem a damning indictment of the current system.[17] In the US, the undemocratic Founding Fathers listened to Aristotle and chose elections. In 2002, a leading global expert on electoral processes, Rafael López Pintor, in his *Voter Turnout Since 1945* report, included a section 'Choosing Politicians by Lottery: An Option for the Future?', where he claimed: 'The arguments for the use of the lot are highly valid today', and goes on to detail several of the contemporary examples listed above.[18]

The most dramatic changes would be the end of politicians as we now know them, the elimination of all political parties and the replacement of elections with an annual, highly anticipated, citizen lottery. We would no longer go to tick or number boxes once every few years – instead we would be glued to a screen wondering if our name, or that of someone we know, would be drawn to legislate for the next five years. The citizen lottery would become a major event that transformed the lives of the several hundred people selected every year to replace the outgoing portions of various local, regional and national parliaments. These people would suddenly be thrust into the political spotlight; how to deal with this would need serious and careful consideration.

Political parties would become just another civil society group, like existing lobbying and interest groups. Electoral campaigns spending millions of dollars and saturating advertising channels (in countries where this is allowed) would cease. There would be no such thing as donations to parties and candidates, or job offers upon retirement. The representatives would not need to court the media behemoths for favourable coverage. And it would be simple to ensure that one parliamentarian comes from each electoral seat so that there is a continuing connection between one member of parliament and a specific constituency (where this is currently the case).

Not that change of this magnitude will come easily. There are many important arguments to be had, addressed below, and, moreover, political battles to be won and alliances to be built. Furthermore, most ordinary people, if selected to govern, would most likely be decidedly nervous about their new position. If a citizen-legislator takes her or his responsibility seriously, then legislating would most likely be a difficult and stressful few years. No one should assume that governing is easy.

This is a very preliminary sketch of a general idea, the precise details of which will be very important – although one notable bonus of sortition is that the idea is relatively easy to communicate. The remainder of this book fleshes out the claims and evidence in support of the legitimacy and viability of sortition, and addresses the moral, practical and strategic implications entailed by such a change.

Notes

1. Fishkin, *People*, 119; see also http://participedia.net/en/methods/deliberative-polling.

2. Sean Gray, *Deliberative Polling*, http://participedia.net/en/methods/deliberative-polling.

3. From www.AmericaSpeaks.org (now closed down). But see, for example, http://www.bancroftandcompany.com/weekly-column/resolving-the-budget-deficit-will-take-more-than-just-cuts.html.

4. Fishkin, *People*, 112.

5. Harm van Dijk and Jerphaas Donner, private communication.

6. Chwalisz, *Populist*, 90.

7. Matthew Flinders, Katie Ghose, Will Jennings, *et al.*, *Democracy Matters: Lessons from the 2015 Citizens' Assemblies on English Devolution* (https://www.electoral-reform.org.uk/file/2717/download?token=dcPseSyF), 40. See also http://citizensassembly.co.uk/.

8. Gutmann and Thompson, *Deliberative Democracy*, 129.

9. Dahl, *Democracy*, 113 (emphasis in original).

10. Gutmann and Thompson, *Deliberative Democracy*, 114.

11. Quoted in Smith, *Innovations*, 73.

12. Smith, *Innovations*, 73. See also Lyn Carson and Brian Martin, *Random Selection in Politics* (Praeger, 1999) and David Van Reybrouck, *Against Elections: The Case for Democracy* (The Bodley Head, 2016).

13. Gutmann and Thompson, *Deliberative Democracy*, 7, 3, 101, 116.

14. Gutmann and Thompson, *Deliberative Democracy*, 80.

15. Phillips, *Presence*, 40.

16. Keane, *Democracy*, 18, 29.

17. Aristotle, *Politics*, 1294b – for example, http://www.perseus.tufts.edu/hopper/text?doc=Perseus:text:1999.01.0058:book=4:section=1294b.

18. López Pintor and Gratschew (eds), *Voter Turnout*, 92.

Chapter 13: Sortition: Competent, Legitimate, Accountable, Viable

Perhaps the most common criticism of the random selection of legislators is that it would not filter out ill-equipped candidates in the way elections supposedly do, or, equivalently, that the vast majority of people lack the skills or intelligence to comprehend and amend laws. Critics may also say that it might work at the small, local scale but could never do so at a national level (or global – heaven forbid!); or that it would be too expensive, or take too much time, or that people do not want to be involved in lawmaking. Then there are the more serious objections: that the people so chosen would lack any political mandate; that elimination of elections – the key to gaining the active consent of the citizenry – would eliminate the fundamental mechanism of political accountability and source of governmental legitimacy; or that such a system would pose irredeemable practical questions about how one would choose an executive, or a president, or other national representatives for international summits and bodies such as the UN, the WTO or the World Bank. Furthermore, is change of this scale feasible, and if so, how? Dismissing the entire project as hopelessly naïve is the easiest way to ignore the appeal of sortition and the relative ease with which most of these criticisms can be addressed. Strategies for achieving such a change are outlined in Part Four below.

Are laws and governmental policies too complex for ordinary people to understand? Are people, on average, too stupid to be able to do so? Does the making and modifying of laws require a minimum level of competence that a randomly selected person would most likely not possess, whereas an elected person most likely would? We would not choose a pilot or surgeon by random selection, so the common analogy goes, so why choose our legislators that way? As Dahl points out, however, this analogy is based on fallacious ideas of the linkages between expert knowledge, competence and the role of government.[1] Government and its officials (especially the police, military, etc.) are the only institutions lawfully allowed to use force to compel coercion of their decisions. When people defer to experts to fly planes, or perform surgery, they have the option to accept or reject their advice and cannot be forced to submit to the experts' decisions (up to the point where we get on the plane or are administered the anaesthetic). There is a fundamental difference between delegating subordinate decisions (over which we have ultimate control) to experts, and handing over responsibility for state power (which will have authority over us). Dahl, and most deliberative democrats, further point out that governing does not require strictly scientific or technical knowledge; the fundamental decisions of allocating finite resources between competing demands are essentially moral decisions. Deliberative processes aim to identify the moral crux of these decisions, so that compromise is made with the full understanding and acknowledgement of any trade-offs.

As Hardt and Negri say:

> Knowledge is obviously a prerequisite for democratic participation and management of the common. But one should not exaggerate the complexity of the knowledges required to engage in political decisions regarding our society... We need today to stimulate the appetite for these knowledges and rediscover the pleasures of political participation.[2]

If elections *did* somehow magically produce qualified experts, the logical conclusion of that assumption would be to submit potential surgeons, pilots and CEOs to an electoral process. Alternately, if expertise is the paramount consideration for obtaining office, then examination may be the best way to determine candidacy. Indeed, it still is for those wishing to work in much of the civil service, and has been used extensively to allocate political authority in China.[3]

A more subtle version of the same argument is that elections are more likely to filter out those manifestly lacking the requisite skills of office. This is not saying elections produce experts, merely that they eliminate fools. However, it is easy to question the implied presumption: that winners of the electoral process are somehow suited to making and amending laws. King and Crewe's *The Blunders of our Governments* details frightening examples of how ignorance, incompetence and the disconnect between elite politicians and the real lives of much of the population can lead to spectacular failures of policy. They argue that ministerial accountability is a myth; ministers may resign over scandals and gaffes but rarely over policy failures.[4] It is far from evident that elections select competent individuals.

Even if lawyers do predominate in politics, the skills required to win electoral competitions (an image that appeals to swinging voters, being charismatic and photogenic, or a great orator, or a ruthless strategist able to construct coalitions by currying favours or having access to networks of wealth) are not the same as those that one would wish legislators to have. The proposal that surviving the vicissitudes of internal party intrigue is somehow like an apprenticeship for the real thing is a sorry reflection on the current state of politics. Popularity in and of itself, especially in a climate where this is not based on a serious appraisal of policies but more on performance and spectacle, would seem a poor metric for governance. 'Contestability refers not only to the existence of real competition in the election of candidates but also to the requirement that the attractiveness of one candidate over another should be driven less by the politics of identity, personality, and patronage and more by issues of public policy,' says Fölscher in the World Bank report mentioned in Chapter 11.[5]

Still it is true, and must be acknowledged, that many people would be ill suited to being in charge of a country's affairs. Most people have a very limited understanding of politics and legislative processes. People are often irrational, apathetic and ignorant. Stupidity, however, is something different. Ignorance can be overcome, apathy reversed. And the alternative to universal inclusion – that we should exclude people from government based on intelligence (or some other measure) – smacks strongly of the reasoning of 'legitimate exclusion' used to justify restricting the vote to rich white men after the French and American revolutions. It would represent an indefensible discrimination violating basic tenets of political equality under random selection – the equal *probability* of being selected for office.

On the use of random selection in ancient Athens, Manin suggests there was 'a deep mistrust of professionalism' in politics: 'The assumption was that if professionals intervened in government they would inevitably dominate.' And so:

> The Athenians, not generally regarded as unsophisticated in political matters, must have been aware that lot appointed people indiscriminately, yet they continued to use the system for two hundred years. The fact that selection by lot risks elevating unqualified citizens to public office is not a modern discovery... Possibly they saw advantages in lot that, all things considered, they felt outweighed this major disadvantage. Possibly, too, they had

found a way of guarding against this risk of incompetence through supplementary institutional arrangements.[6]

The supplementary arrangements Manin highlights include the 'rendering of account' upon leaving office (a public reckoning of a person's performance in office), the use of no-confidence votes, and in particular the voluntary nature of the service. If sortition were instituted, should actual participation in government be voluntary? It is an interesting question, although it would be difficult, and perhaps counterproductive, to make it compulsory, even if compulsory voting in countries such as Australia and Belgium, and compulsory jury duty around the world, has a robust defence in participatory, representative terms. If it were voluntary, perhaps most of those who accepted the position would be motivated and dedicated to the task.

Fortunately, recent experience supports such optimism. The assemblies conducted to date show that large numbers of people, combined with good processes, can produce a surfeit of engaged and thoughtful attendees. A principal argument for having a wide selection of people (say, several hundred) is that a few incompetent (or disruptive, or unmotivated) people would be vastly outnumbered by those 'ready, willing and able' to participate meaningfully.[7] Dryzek states: 'The most obvious finding from mini-publics relevant to the larger public sphere is that, given the opportunity, ordinary citizens can make good deliberators. Moreover, issue complexity is no barrier to the development and exercise of that competence.'[8] Matthew Flinders and his colleagues, who organised two pilot citizens' assemblies in the UK in 2015, concur:

> The findings… do reveal a huge amount about the capacity and potential of men and women… to make a valuable and informed contribution to complex questions of constitutional policy making. They reveal the manner in which people can and will listen and change their minds and how, when faced with the evidence and facts (rather than the stereotypes and mythology), that the public's attitudes can become far more balanced and constructive, possibly even quite positive. That is a critical point. As recent studies have revealed, there is a huge difference between the public's 'quick thinking' in relation to issues of politics and attitudes about politicians (generally aggressive, negative, belligerent, etc.), compared with their 'slow thinking' about the

same issues (far more balanced, empathetic, constructive, etc.). In this sense what citizens' assemblies really seem to offer is a new democratic space that helps nurture or facilitate 'slow thinking'.[9]

Some supporters of sortition, such as French professor of political science Yves Sintomer, worry that if the difference in opinion between participants and non-participants is great, then perhaps the legitimacy of the process will be undermined.[10] However, even classical democratic theory regularly recognises that it is the post-deliberative opinion of people (or politicians) that is important. Mini-publics take this as an explicit aim.

In *The Difference: How the Power of Diversity Creates Better Groups, Firms, Schools and Societies*, Scott Page from the University of Michigan develops a model to explain how and why 'diversity trumps ability' in many instances.[11] He claims that large groups of random people often come up with better solutions to complex problems than groups of experts. Their diversity of world views, problem-solving strategies and perspectives allows them to discover superior solutions, whereas experts tend to apply a more homogenous set of tools that will, in general, lead to one particular outcome. Over a large range of complex problems, this will typically be suboptimal. Page can therefore propose an 'instrumental argument' for diversity in groups: there is no need to base the argument in historical exclusion or increased legitimacy; the simple fact is that diverse groups perform better. Page concludes:

> ... the benefits of diversity do exist. They're not huge. We shouldn't expect them to be huge. But they're real, and over time, if we can leverage them, we'll be far better off. We'll find better solutions to our problems. We'll make better predictions. We'll live in a better place.[12]

Hélène Landemore, in *Democratic Reason: Politics, Collective Intelligence, and the Rule of the Many*, extends these ideas and applies them to democracy, presenting 'a sustained epistemic argument for democracy based on the idea of collective intelligence'.[13] Group intelligence is more than the sum of its parts – the interactions within *diverse* groups generate high-quality solutions to problems. Democracy can therefore be defended as the best form of government from an instrumental point of view: the rule of the many 'is simply a smarter regime than the rest'. It is unnecessary to appeal to humanistic principles of equality or inclusion to argue that democracy is better than aristocracy, monarchy or dictatorship. The many are simply smarter than the few; therefore, democracy is the best form of government.

If the aim of democracy is to make the best collective decisions about complex societal problems, and cognitive diversity is an essential ingredient of group intelligence, Landemore concludes that the form of representation to best achieve this goal is random selection:

> ... a counterintuitive implication of the importance of cognitive diversity for the epistemic performance of a deliberating group is that random selection is preferable to elections as a selection mechanism for representatives. Random selection indeed preserves the cognitive diversity of the larger group, whereas elections will tend to reduce it.[14]

A parliament full of diverse, ordinary people, far from being a cause of concern, will actually produce balanced decisions. They should certainly, according to this research, produce better outcomes than our relatively homogenous current legislatures, especially over extended periods of time and across the wide range of complex problems facing society.

The elitist condemnation of the stupidity of the masses, and their supposed incapacity to govern, is probably the biggest threat to any form of democracy. As Dahl points out:

> The claim that government should be turned over to experts deeply committed to rule for the general good and superior to others in their knowledge of the means to achieve it – Guardians, Plato called them – has always been the major rival to democratic ideas. Advocates of Guardianship attack democracy at a seemingly vulnerable point: they simply deny that ordinary people are competent to govern themselves.[15]

It is precisely this appeal to a necessary guardianship that authoritarian regimes such as China use to justify their control and monopoly of power. If people are too stupid to govern, then perhaps they are also too stupid to vote. This view is what the democratic struggles of the last few centuries have fought to overcome.

The most serious challenge to sortition comes from those proclaiming that it is an illegitimate system whose representatives are not account-able to the people. In this view, elections are seen as, if not the only way, then the principal way by which politicians are held to account.

A related, yet distinct, understanding of the way politicians are held to account is that candidates outline an agenda, and if elected are given a mandate to pursue it. They receive the 'consent of the gov-erned' to pursue their stated policies and if they do not pursue those objectives, or govern poorly, they can be punished by removal from office.

The simple reply to the whereabouts of the locus of consent in sortition is that it shifts. The people consent to be governed by a randomly selected, representative sample of people.[16] The legislative assembly gains its legitimacy from being a representative sample of people deliberating in a fair and informed institution.[17] Such an assembly would supply all the typical 'institutional goods' demanded of a legitimate parliament: the legislature would be inclusive of diverse voices and the people would be in direct control, producing laws after considered judgement of the options and evidence, utilising a trans-parent process.[18] Such a system must assure the wider population that the legislators chosen by sortition are doing as any group of citizens would have done, or indeed what all of them would have done, were that possible. The argument that elections repeatedly and regularly gain the electorate's consent is shallow at best: people never get the chance to reaffirm that they wish to live in an electoral democracy, and if voter turnout is any indication of enthusiasm, this wish is wan-ing.

If a nation wanted to rewrite its constitution, it could consent to give the task to an informed, randomly selected representative assem-bly – as proposed in Chile in 2013. If they wanted to change the elec-toral law, it might do the same, as the province of British Columbia in Canada did in 2004. If the aim is empowered decision-making, and the assembly is considered legitimate – if it is agreed that the process is a simulation of how the entire citizenry would decide under similar conditions – then it should be *guaranteed that the assembly's proposal be directly implemented, especially if it comes from a supermajority*. If the aim is to decide what deliberating people *would* think in fair and informed conditions, then submitting the assembly decisions to a referendum runs directly counter to these deliberative ideals.

Referenda, like elections, are strikingly inferior methods of gauging the informed, justified opinion of citizens. The 2016 Brexit result is the most profound recent outcome of this disconnect. Why people voted the way they did in the referendum has been much discussed: was it immigration, a desire to punish politicians, a generational and educational divide, stagnating living standards or local political factors?[19] The complex issues that influenced people's actions in the voting booth are difficult to disentangle, but the truly profound point is that no one assumes or argues that voting occurred after a serious appraisal of consequences or any attempt to discuss and justify to each other why or how either outcome would address people's concerns. People used the referendum 'to answer a set of questions not printed on the ballot paper'.[20]

Theoretically, parliamentary debates are undertaken specifically to allow representatives to be swayed by the force of other arguments and evidence. Strict forms of accountability are not the ideal in any form of representative democracy, which is why referenda were dismissed by UK politicians until relatively recently. If politicians acted like delegates, and had to do exactly what the majority of voters directed them to do, then public debate and justification would serve little purpose. This is why legislators' decisions are not then put to a referendum – accountability lies not in legislators directly mimicking the opinion of their constituents, but in the act of justifying why it might differ. Similarly, if a citizens' assembly accurately simulates how any sample of informed people would have decided, then its decisions should be publicly justified and directly implemented.

Not that parliamentary debate today lives up to the ideals outlined above. King details 'the deeply flawed manner in which many laws are made in the UK', where 'party competition and antagonisms are almost invariably to the fore' and 'ministers frequently go through the largely cosmetic process of public consultation... [and] there are few parliamentary forums for head-scratching, evidence-taking and extensive discussion and debate'.[21] Committees typically just 'go through the motions' as government control of parliament typically means the outcome of the various readings and votes are usually, although not always, foregone conclusions. Parliaments should be chambers of deliberation and opinion change; at the moment, they most certainly are not.

As stated above, what *should* count is a politician's post-deliberative position, not a campaign promise.[22] Ideally, our legislators are affected by reasoned debate and would, hopefully, even change their positions as a result of argument and evidence. Deliberative democracy posits this ideal as an explicit starting point. As Phillips says: 'Participants in a deliberative democracy have to be freed from stricter forms of political accountability if they are to be freed to engage in discussion.'[23] She points out that to support women's quotas in politics, or a politics of presence in general, is to inevitably distance oneself 'from a politics of binding mandates'.[24] Political representatives are not merely glorified messengers, and accountability is therefore more complex. Sortition takes this point even further: the participants are completely free to engage in meaningful and thoughtful deliberation and are in no way tied to the opinions of their constituents, although they would be expected to provide moral justifications for their decisions.

It is true, as Smith points out in *Democratic Innovations*, that 'random selection undermines our established conceptions of political accountability'.[25] Elections have a stranglehold on our political imaginations. Conceiving of accountability without elections seems difficult, which is surely an artefact of recent history – it was certainly not difficult for the democrats of ancient Athens.

This more sophisticated response to the question of the whereabouts of 'the consent of the governed' in sortition undermines the assumption that elections are fundamental to political accountability. It was detailed in Chapter Four how suspect many of these assumptions are: our politicians are only minimally responsive to their constituents, and mostly only to the wealthiest; parties are under the distorting influence of big money and vested interests; and elections are very blunt instruments to punish hypocrisy or reward good governance.[26]

Many pieces of legislation are voted on in a single term of office, of which only a small subset will have been outlined in an election platform. In countries where electoral systems are dominated by two major parties, the ability to punish is not really an option at all if the other major party is even further from your liking. In those countries with proportional systems, where coalitions of governing parties are commonplace, who then in the coalition should be punished: the largest coalition partner that compromised, or one of the smaller partners making demands?

Between elections, things change. It is impossible to know in advance which issues will come up, and how parliamentarians will deal with them, meaning mandates must necessarily be fluid. In the US, a second-term president does not have to face another election (a two-term limit being an implicit recognition of the dangers of political professionalism) – does the fact that there is no fear of electoral reward or sanction mean the president is free to do as she or he wishes and lacks accountability?

In Australia, at least, detailed mandates are a thing of the past. The conservative Liberal Party's 1993, 650-page 'Fightback!' manifesto is remembered as 'the longest suicide note in political history'; after its publication, the party's leader, John Hewson, lost a supposedly 'unlosable' election.[27] Every leader since has been wary of detailed pre-election articulations of policy.

Important differences in policy do exist between major parties in modern democracies. However, it is easy (indeed necessary if the system is to be portrayed as competitive) to overemphasise them. The so-called 'end of left and right' has been much discussed, and for good reason – across the broad spectrum of economic ideas what is most striking is the excessively narrow range of generally neoliberal policies that our elected representatives are allowed to articulate if they do not want to be mauled by the mainstream media. According to King:

> Britain's main political parties today, for all their detailed policy differences, are closer together than at any time since the 1920s in their broad ideological sweep… Britain's leaders appear determined to strive for dissensus, exaggerating differences that really do exist and inventing ones that do not.'[28]

Just as a well-known strategy of climate change deniers is to overemphasise disputes among climate change scientists, so too will supporters of the democratic status quo overemphasise the differences between major parties. No matter who you vote for, a politician always wins, so it is said. Or, as Herbert Marcuse put it: 'Free election of masters does not abolish the masters or the slaves.'[29]

A media-saturated politics certainly does not encourage the detailed articulation of competing policy options. The power of five-word (or less) sloganeering is well understood, and the power of personalities in the current system more so.[30] In general almost no one, outside the narrow milieu of political hacks (opposition candidates, media pundits, other parties), reads even the minimal policy statements presented.

Do politicians who have broken electoral promises get punished? While it seems true that scandal-wracked governments are often booted out, it also appears that incumbent governments will be blamed for things largely beyond their control – dismissal of parties from all sides of the political spectrum in Europe after the 2008 financial crisis being a case in point. It may be valid to blame governments for poor economic policy leading to recession and high unemployment, but in a world of interlinked and globalised finance that flows freely between nations, the actual portion of blame that should befall governments is highly debatable. In *Democracy for Realists*, Achen and Bartels:

> ... focus on how well citizens are able to assess responsibility for changes in their own welfare. Since there are many realms of politics, economics, and society in which leaders' responsibility for good or bad outcomes is far from clear, we consider cases in which leaders are clearly not responsible for good or bad outcomes – droughts, floods, and shark attacks. We find that voters punish incumbent politicians for changes in their welfare that are clearly acts of God or nature. That suggests that their ability (or their inclination) to make sensible judgments regarding credit and blame is highly circumscribed. In that case, retrospection will be blind, and political accountability will be greatly attenuated.[31]

They continue:

> The primary implication of our analyses of retrospective voting is that election outcomes are mostly just erratic reflections of the current balance of partisan loyalties in a given political system... [E]lections are capricious collective decisions based on considerations that ought, from the viewpoint of the folk theory [of democracy], to be largely irrelevant – and that will, in any case, soon be forgotten by the voters themselves. We conclude that the retrospective model of democracy simply will not bear the normative weight that its proponents want to place on it.[32]

Voters do not reward or punish politicians or parties in any meaningful, consistent or considered way. When voting, 'group and partisan loyalties, not policy preferences or ideologies, are fundamental in democratic politics'.[33] Whatever elections are doing, they are not holding politicians to account.

There are several other reasons to doubt the claim that elections are the principal way politicians are held to account. As outlined above, Keane and Castells show with ample evidence that it is more the network of civil society institutions, coupled with increased transparency rules, and a free and pluralistic media, that keeps politicians in the spotlight, and it was not until after World War II that many of these institutions blossomed.[34] Keane marks this era as the beginning of a *monitory* democracy – a democracy constantly being monitored.[35] Dryzek makes a related point: 'The rise of networked governance undercuts notions of sovereignty and accountability... Traditional aggregative and electoral ideas about democracy are helpless in the face of these developments.' He also points out, in relation to deliberative democracy, that 'accountability can also mean simply being required to give an account justifying decisions and actions, and that can happen without any necessary reference to election campaigns'.[36]

Any credible definition of democracy will detail far more than the mode of selection of legislators. Elections by themselves are not sufficient, as evidenced in many of the most corrupt so-called democracies on the planet.[37] If civil society is weak or non-existent, and the judiciary or media is not independent, elections are easily exploited by power-hungry elites, usually to the great detriment of the people. For any real democracy to flourish, civil liberties and systems of checks and balances between the legislators, civil society, the media and the judiciary are arguably the more important element.

With sortition, all this would continue. Legislators would still be in the spotlight. They would still come before the media to justify their decisions. They would still be expected to govern in the interests and for the good of the country (or city, state or planet) and its people. Transparency of decision-making would still allow an expansive civil society network to monitor and critique proposed or actual laws. The judiciary would still have powers to denounce laws as unconstitutional. Legislators would still be accountable.

But where will the buck stop and who will take responsibility when things go wrong? Would certain members of the assembly feel obligated to resign in the face of unforeseen problems or failures of oversight? Should sortition come with no-confidence votes resulting in replacement if a supermajority of the assembly thinks so? What should happen when corruption is uncovered? These complex questions would need much debate, and hindsight and experience will be important for many of them.

What can be pointed out is that the wealth of evidence from citizens' assemblies demonstrates that participants make 'public-spirited judgements' and 'generally do feel a sense of responsibility to the wider public interest, take their responsibility seriously, and act *as if* they were being held to account'.[38] Randomly selected people in the assemblies held to date are typically highly committed and enthusiastic, and try to make decisions for the common good. This is all good news for sortition.

'What ordinary people lack in knowledge, they make up in freedom', says the Belgian G1000 manifesto. The final report continues:

> Each stage of the G1000 confirmed our suspicion: ordinary citizens are not only willing to think about political issues; they are also capable of doing so. If they are given enough space, information and a rigorous methodology to work with, ordinary citizens can come up with constructive solutions; even for complex or emotionally charged issues. If one is taken seriously, one will respond to that seriously.[39]

Ultimately, when constituting these assemblies, the question is not what human nature is, but what it can become under certain, highly artificial conditions; this is a project to bring a different kind of politics into existence.[40]

Nevertheless, most of the deliberative assemblies mentioned above have had their agenda set by external agents (the Dutch G1000s being a notable exception). Under sortition, who would introduce new legislation or decide which laws are to be amended? Currently, majority parties, or coalitions of parties, craft policies that are translated into legislation. What would be the process when parties no longer exist? Some mechanism for the transmission of concerns from the people to the legislators needs to exist.

There are several solutions to this problem. In ancient Greece, a council of randomly selected citizens (the *boule*) drafted the legislation to be presented to the open assembly. A rotating executive could perform a similar function in the system outlined above. Or it could be left to the initiative of the entire assembly; agenda-setting sessions could become a regular part of the process, as happens in the Dutch G1000s.

In general, the framing of issues and setting of agendas is a complex societal process whereby lobbying groups, civil society, the media and public opinion all play important roles. As happens now, especially outside electoral periods, legislators react to and are influenced by the media and perceived public concerns, and this would continue to be the case.

In a highly networked society, it is arguably easier for citizens to raise concerns, and there are some exciting experiments in empowered agenda-setting being conducted by several of the large online campaigning groups, in particular at Avaaz.org. Once a year they let their membership determine which issues to prioritise by conducting an all-member poll. Individual campaign ideas are then refined by conducting 10,000-member random sample polls, leading to member-driven campaign strategies. An expanding array of online deliberative tools could be used not only to vote for various issues to be high priority, but also actively to discuss them and try to justify propositions.[41] It would indeed be an interesting, participatory and network democracy if the population at large decided upon the agenda for randomly selected parliamentarians to address through informed deliberation on everybody's behalf.

There is at least one important caveat here: any polling must also involve a stratified random sample, as open online forums suffer the same problems of self-selection that open public forums suffer. Participants in online open meetings, as in open public meetings, are typically the most vocal, committed and evangelical, and will rarely represent the community at large. Random sampling is the solution to issues such as these.

Guaranteeing and expanding civil liberties is perhaps the best way to ensure members of the assembly are listening to the people. Obvious signs that legislators are *not* tracking public priorities and concerns, such as masses of people protesting on the streets and in the squares, are then easy to spot.

Beyond these important debates about competence, legitimacy and accountability there is an array of practical considerations, especially concerning the role of experts, bureaucrats and facilitators, and how to allocate high-level posts such as presidents or prime ministers.

Access to expert information is very important. Yet experts are fallible and biased, and predictions fail, as the 2008 economic crisis forcefully demonstrated. As Chang points out in his chapter 'Good Economic Policy Does Not Require Good Economists', during the miracle years of economic development in much of South East Asia 'economists were in fact conspicuous by their absence'.[42] Daniel Kahneman details 'the illusion of skill' among wealth advisors, who he found were 'rewarding luck as if it were skill' due largely to their 'sincere overconfidence'.[43]

You do not need to be an expert epidemiologist or microbiologist to know we should have hygiene standards in food factories, butchers' shops and restaurants. Expert lawyers and professionals will be needed to flesh out the details of our laws, but they must be subordinate to our legislators, whose principal aim should be articulating precise goals and methods of achieving agreed moral outcomes in broadly understandable language.

As has been recognised at least since John Dewey pointed it out in 1927: 'A class of experts is inevitably so removed from common interests as to become a class with private interests and private knowledge, which in social matters is not knowledge at all.'[44] There are systemic processes that bind expert knowledge to special interests. However, policy choices should not be made on the basis of incorrect or outdated facts; knowing where expert opinion lies and where disagreement exists, and having the detailed results of peer-reviewed studies of policy outcomes, must inform political choice. Experts should be on tap, but never on top.

Giving experts, facilitators and bureaucrats a prominent role in the assemblies is obviously an area where bias and influence must be checked. Would we be accidentally instituting a dictatorship of the facilitators and experts? People's experience of 'expert witnesses' in courts of law who are called to justify almost any point of view, without any verification that what they are saying is unbiased, has undermined the notion of the independent expert.

Organiser bias – the bias of experts, facilitators and other organisers of deliberative forums – will always be present to some extent. Carson, a key organiser of the Australian Citizens' Parliament, documents 'the impossibility of neutrality' in such a forum, and advocates transparency and *open deliberation about bias itself* to develop the awareness and critical capacities of the participants to identify and deal with organiser bias.[45] The participants themselves should probably have much input into the selection of expert witnesses, and of course be able to challenge or ignore information as they see fit.

A dedication to organiser independence is critical. The various departments and institutions providing organisers and experts must rigorously pursue and enforce impartiality, as far as possible, as they prepare for and fulfil their specific roles. Examples of how to do this exist in many professions using a variety of peer review, requisite training and qualifications, feedback and evaluation. The process can be symbolised by the taking of a public oath, whereby the experts and facilitators swear to uphold principles of neutrality and disinterest. Examples of the kinds of information experts would be allowed to present to an assembly can usefully be taken from the three core Wikipedia policies: the information must be verifiable, it must not be original research (only research already published in credible, peer-reviewed journals) and it must be presented from a neutral point of view. Presentations on background and alternative policy options could be screened by multiple peers to satisfy these conditions, and an independent body for the evaluation, selection and accreditation and upholding of professional standards could be instituted. This process would be difficult, and should be transparent and continually open to challenge and improvement, as it is easy to foresee complex, and necessary, debates similar in nature to those around the current processes for selecting the judiciary in many countries. There is little doubting the contentious nature of this important process.

At every table in these deliberative assemblies the role of facilitator is also crucial. Although she or he should not direct the content of deliberations, they should ensure that everyone's voice is heard, call for dominating voices to be curtailed and facilitate an understanding of potential bias and the differences between moral (i.e., mutually justifiable) reasoning and other speech acts. What this entails in practice will also be an ongoing debate, and Phillips points out that strict demands for rational discussion can privilege certain people and therefore undermine equality of access for participants.[46] The balance between too strict and too liberal facilitation is difficult to achieve, and will be an ongoing area of concern.[47] Ensuring high standards of professional facilitation will be important and demanding. Each table could have the right to request a new facilitator, or possibly request none, and accusations of bias or interference by a facilitator would have to be taken very seriously. The good news is that in nearly every example to date, facilitators are commonly perceived as being neutral and efficient – in the UK pilot citizens' assemblies in 2015, approximately 90 per cent of participants thought the facilitators upheld standards of neutrality and equality of access.[48]

The ideal to strive for is self-facilitation, whereby everyone around a table has the wherewithal and experience to keep on topic, stop themselves from dominating discussions or speak up if shy. In this case, the facilitator would almost be a silent observer, tracking contributions and the quality of deliberation. In the AmericaSpeaks model mentioned above, a 'theme team' also has considerable influence, as they are responsible for selecting the common topics and issues flowing in from all the tables simultaneously. As with experts and facilitators, clear standards should be articulated, peer review probably instituted and thorough mechanisms put in place to ensure independence.

Advisors, bureaucrats and parliamentary staff have much power in our current system. They often write speeches, produce publicity, liaise with the media and necessarily develop contacts and networks with staff of other parliamentarians and civil servants. Placing politically inexperienced people in their midst could lead to attempted manipulation. At a minimum, incoming randomly selected citizens would require much assistance and comprehensive training. It may take several months to introduce them to parliamentary and legislative procedures, the available resources, ethical concerns, the current debates and the structure of existing laws, to name but a few areas of induction. Like current politicians, they would have paid staff, perhaps selected from a pool of experienced personnel, to help them navigate the system and assist in research, organisation, media liaison and the like. Potentially, those parliamentarians in their final year, or those who have finished their five-year term, could mentor and advise those in their first year. In any case, a combination of rigorous screening, evaluation and training of parliamentary staff to recognise and deal with bias, or interference, would also be needed.

Several other issues fall into the broad category of practical difficulties. Can the process work at the level of a nation state? Are the costs of holding deliberative forums too high? How would a prime minister or president be selected, and who would represent the government in international bodies?

'Size matters,' claims Dahl about democracy. Direct democracy, he says, requires small scales, while 'the absence of a strong common identity' makes it 'highly unlikely' that representative democracy would ever be extended beyond the nation-state.[49] This could be called the Goldilocks Hypothesis: the (relatively recent) invention of the nation state created conditions that are 'just right' for our current form of democracy; larger contexts would be too large because of the overwhelming diversity, and in smaller contexts more direct forms of democracy, such as town meetings, could be used. These claims are highly suspect. There are many examples of culturally diverse states that are thriving democracies, from the limited diversity of multi-lingual Switzerland, to the extraordinary diversity of India or Papua New Guinea, where several hundred languages are spoken.[50] Indeed, the US should soon become a nation of minorities, with non-Hispanic whites expected to make up less than half of the population by 2050 (down from 80 per cent in 1980[51]), and few are predicting the death of democracy in the US because of these changes. Demographics and diversity are not in and of themselves impossible challenges to democracy on any scale. Hardt and Negri point out that:

> Advocates of democracy in early modern Europe and North America were confronted by sceptics who told them that democracy may have been possible in the confines of the Athenian *polis* but was unimaginable in the extended territories of the modern nation states. Today, advocates of democracy in the age of globalization are met by sceptics who claim democracy may have been possible within the confines of the national territory but is unimaginable on a global scale.[52]

Democracy, and sortition, can work at any scale, from the local to the provincial and the national, and even on a global level. However, to function globally, selection would require every nation to respect fundamental democratic freedoms and civil liberties. Global legislators would have to be free from punitive repercussions at home if they disobey powerful national bodies and groups. This is obviously a fantasy in our current system of powerful nation states, where around half are authoritarian regimes, but global issues such as trade, immigration and climate change could be effectively addressed if such a forum were empowered to do so.

Concerns about the excessive cost of large deliberative forums are irrelevant to the proposal to replace electoral democracy with sortition. There would be no extra long-term expenses involved in replacing our legislatures of elected politicians with a random sample of people. Indeed, it would probably be significantly cheaper, since government funding of political parties (where this occurs), and the holding of elections, which cost significant sums of money, would be eliminated.

Who would form the governing executive and head the ministries responsible for the day-to-day running of the state bureaucracies in such a system? With regards to ministers, King is scathing of the current lack of experience and continuity of politicians holding ministerial posts in the UK. Ministers typically come to these posts with little practical experience, and with frequent cabinet reshuffling many stay for an extremely limited time, making the acquisition of knowledge and experience difficult – 'government by neophyte remains broadly the rule', he laments.[53] In some European countries, such as France, the Netherlands and Sweden, ministers are *not allowed* to be members of parliament. There is very little evidence that winning an election produces suitably qualified ministers, and there are many arguments for giving the positions to better-qualified and more experienced individuals. Crucial oversight could be maintained by a randomly selected, rotating and one-year-term executive, as occurred in ancient Athens.[54]

How would one appoint a president or prime minister? One option would be to turn it into a largely symbolic, ceremonial role, as is the case with the presidents of Austria and Italy. The president or prime minister could be elected from and by the random parliamentarians, and would surely be one of their most articulate, well known and respected. Presumably, she or he would have already served some years in parliament, and the possibility of recall and delegated decision-making may be important.

The processes for selecting delegates to participate in international bodies could be left as they are, with crucial parliamentary oversight. Whatever the agreed institutional arrangements, there is no reason to see these issues as insurmountable challenges to sortition. They could, perhaps, profitably be left to a randomly selected citizens' assembly to decide.

If sortition were instituted, what would become of upper houses (often called senates) in bicameral parliaments? Would a house of review be needed? The Power Inquiry in the UK found that 67 per cent of survey respondents thought the fate of the House of Lords should be decided by 'a group of ordinary voters... selected as a jury'.[55] A less radical version of the proposal to completely replace elections with sortition is that *only* the senate be replaced by randomly selected citizens. Van Reybrouck has said: 'If representation of the people can adopt various shapes, why would Parliament not be able to consist of a chamber of elected citizens and of a Senate of allotted citizens?'[56] His book, *Against Elections*, details many such proposals to replace one of the legislative assemblies in a bicameral parliament with an allotted assembly. It also formed the basis of a proposal made in the late 1990s by the UK think-tank Demos for reform of the House of Lords. The newDemocracy Foundation suggests a similar change for the Australian Senate, and Erik Olin Wright has, in *Envisioning Real Utopias*, made a comparable proposal for the US.[57] This may make sense strategically, as a first step, so that people can experience sortition and gain confidence that it works. But it should not be the end point. Why only allow ordinary people to 'keep the bastards honest', as the long-lived slogan of the Australian Democrats, who had members in the Australian Senate for 30 years, claimed?[58] Let us get rid of 'the bastards' altogether and let the people decide. That is what democracy originally entailed, and in the 21st century we have the technology and capacity to achieve it on the scale of nations and beyond. In a truly representative system, no senate is required – although if its purpose is to protect the rights of individual states in a federation, and people continue to consider this important, then a randomly selected senate could also be instituted. Another option would be for a 'double check' to be carried out, whereby vote counts in a unitary legislative chamber include a second count to ensure that a majority of representatives from each state agree.

If it is true, as Churchill famously claimed, 'that democracy is the worst form of Government except all those other forms that have been tried', then our principal measure of the efficacy of sortition over electoral democracy is not if it would be perfect, but if it would be less bad.[59] Sortition is not a panacea, but the freedom of random selection should drastically reduce the capture and distortion of our political system by powerful groups. Money and the need for donations would cease to disrupt the selection process. Political parties would become mere lobby groups. If half of parliament were composed of women, had many young adults and was dominated by people from working-class backgrounds, it would produce very different legislation. Policy would progress along moral lines instead of ideological ones. Difficult issues would be addressed, and sorted out, with sortition.

Notes

1. Dahl, *Democracy*, 71.

2. Hardt and Negri, *Declaration*, 70.

3. Manin, *Principles*, 137.

4. Anthony King and Ivor Crewe, *The Blunders of our Governments* (Oneworld, 2013).

5. Fölscher, 'Participatory', in Shah (ed.), *Participatory*, 248.

6. Manin, *Principles*, 32, 10.

7. Flinders, Ghose, Jennings, *et al.*, *Democracy Matters*, 3.

8. Dryzek with Niemeyer, *Foundations*, 158. See also Lyn Carson, *Ignorance and Inclusion, Mr Jefferson, Might be Good for Democracy* (Working Paper series – United States Studies Centre, University of Sydney, Australia, 2009).

9. Flinders, Ghose, Jennings, *et al.*, *Democracy Matters*, 56.

10. Yves Sintomer, 'Random Selection, Republican Self-Government, and Deliberative Democracy', *Constellations*, 2010, Vol. 17, No. 3, 472–87.

11. Page, *Difference*, 10, 137, 328.

12. Page, *Difference*, 335.

13. Hélène Landemore, *Democratic Reason: Politics, Collective Intelligence, and the Rule of the Many* (Princeton University Press, 2012), 1, 7.

14. Landemore, *Democratic Reason*, 117.

15. Dahl, *Democracy*, 69.

16. Alex Zakaras, 'Lot and Democratic Representation: A Modest Proposal', *Constellations*, 2010, Vol. 17, No. 3, 462; and Manin, *Principles*, 85.

17. Dryzek with Niemeyer, *Foundations*, 21, and Chapter Two in general presents a clear outline of the issue of legitimacy.

18. Smith, *Innovations*, 6, and Chapter Two, especially 12–14.

19. This is but a tiny sample of the analysis: http://blogs.lse.ac.uk/politicsandpolicy/explaining-the-vote-for-brexit/; http://www.independent.co.uk/voices/brexit-theresa-may-when-article-50-why-did-people-vote-wages-housing-market-young-people-a7141206.html; http://www.ft.com/cms/s/2/fe5c6b4e-32f8-11e6-bda0-04585c31b153.html#axzz4JkQmFooP; http://www.newstatesman.com/politics/staggers/2016/07/four-ways-anti-immigration-vote-won-referendum-brexit; http://www.resolutionfoundation.org/publications/the-important-of-place-explaining-the-characteristics-underpinning-the-brexit-vote-across-different-parts-of-the-uk/.

20. Jonathan Freedland, 'A Day of Complete Despair for the 48%', *Guardian Weekly*, 1 July 2016.

21. King, *Britain*, 241–50, quotes are from 250 and 245.

22. Hayward, 'Making Interest', Shapiro *et al.* (eds), *Representation*, 120.

23. Phillips, *Presence*, 156–60 has an interesting discussion on accountability, legitimacy and the connection of a politics of presence with deliberative democracy.

24. Phillips, *Presence*, 56, 80, 149, 163–4.

25. Smith, *Innovations*, 191, also 92.

26. On punishing and rewarding, see the discussion of the 'agency problem' in politics in Ferejohn and Rosenbluth, 'Electoral Representation', in Shapiro *et al.* (eds), *Representation*, 273–7.

27. http://www.theage.com.au/comment/fearful-leaders-cant-see-voters-seek-truth-20130902-2t10i.html.

28. King, *Britain*, 75.

29. Herbert Marcuse, *One-Dimensional Man: Studies in the Ideology of Advanced Industrial Society* (Beacon Press, 1964). See, for example, http://www.marxists.org/reference/archive/marcuse/works/one-dimensional-man/ch01.htm.

30. For example, Obama's 2012 slogan, 'Change we can believe in', and the accompanied chant of 'Yes we can'. Or in Australia, Howard's, and later Abbott's, 'Turn back the boats' in regards to the supposed wave of refugees coming by boat to Australia.

31. Achen and Bartels, *Democracy for Realists*, 15.

32. Achen and Bartels, *Democracy for Realists*, 16.

33. Achen and Bartels, *Democracy for Realists*, 18.

34. See references Chapters Six to Eight.

35. See references in Chapter Three.

36. Dryzek with Niemeyer, *Foundations*, 15, 11.

37. Paul Collier, *Wars, Guns and Votes: Democracy in Dangerous Places* (Bodley Head, 2009).

38. John Parkinson, *Deliberating in the Real World: Problems of Legitimacy in Deliberative Democracy* (Oxford University Press, 2006), 80, quoted in Smith, Innovations, 97–8 (emphasis in original).

39. Derenne *et al.*, *G1000*, 14, 7.

40. Hardt and Negri, *Commonwealth*, 191; and Hardt and Negri, *Multitude*, 212.

41. For example, http://yourview.org, http://liquidfeedback.org (used by various EU Pirate Parties), and many others.

42. Chang, *23 Things*, 244.

43. http://www.nytimes.com/2011/10/23/magazine/dont-blink-the-hazards-of-confidence.html?pagewanted=all&_r=0.

44. Quoted in Sintomer, 'Random Selection', 482.

45. Lyn Carson, 'Investigation of (and Introspection on) Organizer Bias', in Lyn Carson, John Gastil *et al.* (eds), *The Australian Citizens' Parliament and the Future of Deliberative Democracy* (Penn State University Press, 2013).

46. Phillips, *Presence*, 162.

47. Smith, *Innovations*, 84, 87–8, and 146 for the 'theme team' in AmericaSpeaks events.

48. Flinders, Ghose, Jennings, *et al.*, *Democracy Matters*, 39.

49. Dahl, *Democracy*, 105, 116–17. See also Gutmann and Thompson, *Deliberative Democracy*, 31 for a discussion on 'the disadvantages of direct democracy'.

50. Keane, *Democracy*, 585, 676.

51. http://www.bloomberg.com/news/2013-06-13/white-share-of-u-s-population-drops-to-historic-low.html.

52. Hardt and Negri, *Multitude*, 237–8.

53. King, *Britain*, 176, but see also 165, 169, 174–9.

54. Keane, *Democracy*, 890. Note 19 gives many details about this executive in ancient Athens.

55. http://web.archive.org/web/20070704030028/
http://www.makeitanissue.org.uk/OmPolitical.pdf.

56. Derenne *et al.*, *G1000*, 97; see also assignment by lot: 95.

57. Anthony Barnett and Peter Carty, *The Athenian Option: Radical Reform for the House of Lords* (Imprint Academic, 2008);
http://www.newdemocracy.com.au/alternatives/structural/item/98-a-citizens-senate; Erik Olin Wright, *Envisioning Real Utopias* (Verso, 2010).

58. In Argentina '*Que se vayan todas!*' ('Throw them all out!') was a popular chant after the 2001 debt crisis.

59. Quoted in Keane, *Democracy*, 581.

Chapter 14: The End of Politicians

None of the previous material addresses the crucial question of whether it is at all possible to achieve such radical change. Will it ever happen, when political systems change so rarely and there are so many powerful vested interests that would prefer the status quo? Rational argument has never been enough to produce change; it is the distribution and relations of power that usually determine outcomes. Furthermore, what about justice? Would the legislatures be, in general, progressive, or would the laws they produce simply accelerate the levels of inequality within our nation states and across the globe? These important questions, and a discussion of the opportunities and strategies for achieving change, form the topics of Part Four.

The shift to sortition can also be framed as only the first step towards even deeper democracy. The crucial element of this step is breaking the hold of career politicians and political parties on the system, and the hold of elections on our imaginations. Phillips claims that: 'Changing the... composition of elected assemblies is largely an enabling condition... a shot in the dark.'[1] Once a truly representative sample of people have the reins of power, no one can really know what will be enabled. Will another democratic phase towards coordinated decentralisation occur, whereby the hold of centralised bureaucracies is tackled, and sortition is dispersed and pushed down and out to local levels and across all areas where people must decide how to manage and distribute shared and common resources? Most resource decisions are not in the hands of legislatures, and globalised corporations increasingly flaunt national attempts to regulate their exploits, so the larger frontier to cross is perhaps economic and workplace democracy. No democracy is ever perfect; there will always be a better democracy to come, or, as Keane puts it: 'democracy is a process... always on the move... a set of actions that are always in rehearsal... Democracy must always become democracy again.'[2]

Keane also states his vision that 'although citizens and representatives require institutions to govern, *no body should rule*'.[3] Hardt and Negri apparently share this ideal of 'appropriating and subverting "governance without government" as a concept of democracy and revolution'.[4] Perhaps it will be learned that the elimination of rulers does not imply the elimination of rules, and that a truly free society can govern itself.

There are precedents for the obsolescence and disappearance of certain classes of professionals, as technological and cultural change progresses. With the invention of moveable type and the printing press, scribes became irrelevant as books became mass-produced. But instead of calling all these newly empowered printers 'scribes', the term simply disappeared. With blogs and our network revolution anyone can now be a journalist: what Shirky calls 'mass amateurization' is breaking down the exclusive definition of what was once called a media professional; legislative bodies struggle over how to incorporate bloggers into modern media laws and press regulations.[5]

Shirky says: 'Our social tools have been increasingly giving groups the power to coalesce and act in political arenas. We are seeing these tools progress from coordination to governance.'[6] In the same way that 'individual weblogs are not merely alternate sites of publishing – they are alternatives to publishing itself' – so too are deliberative forums not merely alternatives sites of politics, but alternatives to politics itself.[7] As newspapers and traditional media are only now comprehending that it is not competition but obsolescence they are facing, so too politicians do not face competition, they now increasingly face obsolescence.

Flinders notes:

> ... critics are concerned that citizens' assemblies may in fact undermine traditional representative institutions. If a citizens' assembly is a good way of dealing with one issue, citizens might question why is it not a good way to deal with other political issues. Members might contrast the quality of their own discussions with that of the parliamentary debates that they see on television and find their political representatives wanting.[8]

Indeed they might! Which is why it is no wonder there is 'an uneasy feeling among politicians' who observe citizens' assemblies, and that 'often elected representatives can feel threatened by these new initiatives', or that 'people [are] becoming **confused about the role of politicians** in the process'.[9] These feelings are expressed for good reason.

Who will be disappointed if the expensive electoral competition for power and influence disappears, and the media spectacle and millions of dollars flowing between private benefactors and political parties cease, other than those who feed or work in the zoo of our current political system, or benefit inordinately from its persistence?

Will professional career politicians disappear, and the term 'politician', like the term 'scribe', become an artefact, to be studied in history departments?

We can only hope.

Or more: we can actively strive to make it happen.

Notes

1. Phillips, *Presence*, 83.

2. Keane, *Democracy*, 867.

3. Keane, *Democracy*, 856 (emphasis in original).

4. Hardt and Negri, *Commonwealth*, 372.

5. Shirky, *Everybody*, 59.

6. Shirky, *Everybody*, 66.

7. Shirky, *Everybody*, 292.

8. Flinders, Ghose, Jennings, *et al.*, *Democracy Matters*, 41.

9. Derenne *et al.*, *G1000*, 104; OECD, *Focus on Citizens*, 304 and 17 (bold emphasis in the original).

Part IV: Time to Change

'Of course, no honest person claims that happiness is *now* a normal condition among adult human beings; but perhaps it *could* be made normal, and it is upon this question that all serious political controversy really turns.'

–George Orwell, 'Politics vs. Literature: An Examination of Gulliver's Travels'

'Today's Utopia is the flesh and blood of tomorrow.'

–Victor Hugo, *Les Misérables*

Chapter 15: What Is the Good Life?

What kind of society do you want to live in? How should a community of individuals, of which you are but one, pursue happiness collectively? How should society decide who gets what, when and how?[1] What is the good life?

These questions are as old as human society. Democracy's response is that adults should answer them together, as equals: the good life is one where everyone freely and collectively decides what the good life is, while acknowledging that the citizens of tomorrow might disagree.

The proposal that we should institute sortition to select our legislatures stems from the claim that electoral democracy does not satisfy the condition above, and never has. The theoretical equality of 'one person, one vote' is a false equality in practice. Electoral democracy is not a real democracy; the people do not rule. An election is an essentially elitist construction that delivers power into the hands of an unrepresentative assembly dominated by people of wealth and privilege. The following chapters examine the strategies for instituting sortition, and the implications of such a change for progress and justice.

Not that we should imagine that sortition is a terminus in the quest for a better democracy, where societal harmony will prevail for evermore. Fundamental moral disagreement will *always* exist in a free and pluralistic society where diversity is at least respected, and perhaps even encouraged. Any group seeking to impose its own comprehensive moral philosophy on an entire society should be rejected as totalitarian, and rightly so. Interestingly, in the debate about whether legitimacy should stem from an overarching principle of what is good, or arise through the application of a specific process, deliberative democracy takes a middle path. It is neither a purely moral theory (such as utilitarianism, communitarianism, etc.) espousing a single criterion to judge all disagreement, nor is it a purely procedural theory (such as majoritarian theories) proposing a single process by which we should make our decisions. Weaving between these poles, it posits that a certain process (deliberation) that encapsulates certain moral values (non-discrimination, accommodation, mutual respect) can produce legitimate decisions. The theory includes both substantive and procedural principles while denying that either is morally neutral; rather than purging political discourse of disagreement, it searches for ways to foster respect for the moral differences that give rise to it. It is not the end of social conflict, but the ability to address and transform it peacefully and productively.[2] Deliberation seeks to identify the fundamental moral values underlying policy choices and make decisions that acknowledge the possibility of future challenge and change to those decisions.[3]

Having a solid basis in theory is all well and good, but theory will not close the widening chasm between theoretical political equality and increasing economic inequality – which is especially pernicious since the latter seriously undermines the former.

The historical struggle between people demanding political equality, and those with wealth and power determined to maintain their position of privilege, has produced the current crop of electoral democracies. In this fight, the fundamental break from hereditary power to people power was so profound that the question of election versus sortition seemed a minor point.[4] As a result, our occasional vote lends legitimacy to the elites, who then bargain among themselves – influenced, and broadly constrained, by corporations, the media, civil society and the electorate. These elites determine the laws that bind us, with the resulting implications for how society should live together. Elite bargaining is certainly better than hereditary privilege, and much better than war between factions. The institutionalisation of a non-violent forum where the powerful horse-trade for a majority compromise is certainly better than royal decree, aristocratic procla-mation, totalitarian imposition or imperial plunder.

But is electoral democracy the best that can be achieved? Legit-imacy is the key. In 1957, Anthony Downs's influential work argued that 'a political party's primary goal is to win elections and not, as was generally supposed, to enact specific policy initiatives'.[5] Václav Havel, the first post-communist president of Czechoslovakia, elo-quently described 'the nature of the temptation that power represents' as including 'the natural longing every human being has for self-affir-mation'. He struggled 'to imagine a more attractive way to affirm your own existence and its importance than the way offered by politi-cal power'.[6] Certainly, many politicians may be motivated by a vision of a better society, and they will profess publicly that it is this that dri-ves them, but if Havel is correct, then the needs of the ego are not far behind, and the onerous demands of electoral democracy mean a politician's principal struggle will be to keep or obtain a position of power.

The clamour against partisan politicking and the cynicism of the electorate towards politicians of every stripe indicate that this is a very commonly held view, which obviously detracts from the perceived legitimacy of legislative decisions. It is easy to suspect that politicians are only doing what important financial or institutional backers demand so they can remain in power. The path to greater levels of legitimacy is clear, as detailed in Chapter Eleven, and the recent use, by a few governments, of random, representative samples of citizens to deliberate on policy or electoral or constitutional reform point to the possibility of achieving it.

Legitimacy should not be confused with consensus. Everyone need not agree with each other on points of policy. Everyone, however, should agree that the decisions are legitimate, that alternative views have been heard, the discussion has been fair and that everyone has made an effort to accommodate difference. However, it is striking how often deliberative processes result in consensus decisions, or at least supermajority support. Participants, and facilitators in particular, need to be wary that this is not a case of groupthink or peer pressure, but the result of genuine improvements in understanding both the issues and other people's responses to them.

Permanent minorities will, at least, have seats in any such assembly and their voices will be heard, and the hope is that through deliberation their perspective will be incorporated into outcomes; at a bare minimum deliberation requires an acknowledgement of their views. Non-voting seats in an assembly could further be given to resident non-citizens, so that all adults affected by the laws of a state at least have a voice (and non-voting seats would highlight their disempowered position). These possibilities would further increase the legitimacy of the legislatures.

This project can easily be framed as a bipartisan one. There is no a priori guarantee, if the multitude decides upon policy collectively and deliberatively, that the outcomes will be either generally progressive or conservative. What they will produce (if done well) is a decision that reflects an outcome everyone would have come to if it were feasible for every person to be well informed and for them to deliberate together. Random sampling to select legislative representatives should, unlike now, give people a reason to trust those making the decisions. They will, after all, be just like you and me. Someone in that parliament will have your age, someone else your education or income level, and another will be from your area. They will have been plumbers, teachers or sales staff, with the occasional doctor, lawyer or manager. After serving a five-year term, she or he will go back to normal life, and – who knows? – maybe you will be selected to serve next. This should not be a recipe for increased levels of apathy. Even as it removes the act of voting, it replaces it with something sorely lacking in politics: the possibility of empathy.

There will still be decisions people disagree with. Civil society will continue to flourish. Uproar, outrage and protest will continue to occur. It will still be up to all of us, and an active civil society and independent media, to scrutinise decisions and work to guarantee moral outcomes that address and correct injustices. In our current climate, this is an urgent necessity.

Notes

1. Keane, *Democracy*: this is his favourite phrase for describing the fundamental purpose of democracy – for example, xii, 109, 120, etc.

2. Hardt and Negri, *Commonwealth*, 376.

3. Gutmann and Thompson, *Deliberative Democracy*, 91, 94, 123, 126–7, 131. See also 152 for a description of reciprocity; and 57 for the moral and political provisionality of decisions.

4. Manin, *Principles*, 91.

5. Amadae, *Rationalizing*, 137.

6. Václav Havel, http://www.vaclavhavel.cz/ showtrans.php?cat=projevy&val=285_aj_projevy.html&typ=HTML.

Chapter 16: From Here to There

Can electoral democracy be transformed into a democracy based on sortition? If it can, how would it be done? What are the strategies we need to employ to get from here to there?

While acknowledging that different tactics and strategies will work depending on the differing cultural milieux in which the wide variety of democratic practices have arisen across the globe, there are still at least two general and broad strategies for initial consideration: normalising the idea and practice of sortition – for example, by the building of alternatives – and further delegitimising the current system. Campaigning for change in general involves promoting a feasible solution to a compelling problem; knowing when to promote the solution, and when to focus on the problem, is part of a campaigner's art.[1]

Delegitimising the current system is probably the easiest tactic, as politicians and parties do it so well themselves, and the media thrives on scandal. Keeping politicians on the lower end of the ranking of trustworthiness and respect should not be difficult given the widespread cynicism and perception of politics as a field full of ego-driven personal rivalries, and the regular exposition of hypocrisy, corruption and sleaze. Membership of political parties has plummeted, and they are, in general, not highly regarded. For most people, it is easy to guess the answer to the question: 'If ten thousand dollars is to be donated to a group to make the world a better place, should it be given to a charity or a political party?' To continue delegitimising politicians and political parties, support must be given to those who highlight the obscene amounts of money spent on election campaigns, exposing the sources of those funds and the close ties between parties and the mainstream media – as shown, for example, by the Leveson Inquiry in the UK. The lack of women in politics is regularly highlighted; extending this focus to the lack of other under-represented groups could also be done.

It is strange, given how much politicians are disparaged, that elections, the process responsible for their selection, seem largely immune to criticism. Delegitimising the electoral process by emphasising its aristocratic nature will be more difficult. Yet it is obvious that modern electoral systems necessarily produce political-party machines, within which politicians and internal factions struggle for power. Is it due to a failure of imagination? Without a feasible alternative, many may view elections as the only legitimate process, and therefore seek the cause of democracy's problems, or potential solutions, elsewhere. What is needed is a push to undermine elections, to highlight how they necessarily produce biased, demographically unrepresentative assemblies no matter what the funding arrangements or rules are, and that they are, as Aristotle pointed out, the tools of oligarchs. In his 2016 pro-sortition book, *Against Elections*, Van Reybrouck understands where the battle lies. He rails against 'electoral fundamentalism' and the 'blind faith in the ballot box', pointing out the absurdity of using the very private act of voting as a basis for determining how a society should live together:

> Isn't it bizarre that voting, our highest civic duty, boils down to an individual action performed in the silence of the voting booth? Is this really the place where we turn individual gut feelings into shared priorities? Is it really where the common good and the long term are best served?[2]

Justification should be an essential component of politics. Decisions about how to live together should emerge from deliberative, informed discussions. Elections are not the only way, nor the best way, to do democracy. According to Van Reybrouck, they are not 'the Holy Grail of democracy', but 'a poisoned chalice that was deliberately set up as an anti-democratic device'.[3]

The question of election boycotts is a vexed one. Obviously, if very few people vote, the legitimacy of parliament will be easy to question. However, this level of disengagement is probably unlikely to occur: protest or populist parties often rise to snatch the votes of the disenchanted. The system may even continue largely unconcerned by low levels of electoral turnout. Rather, elections should be widely and roundly critiqued, ridiculed and engaged with subversively: demonstrating outside of, or occupying, voting booths may provoke debate; dressing as zombies or armies of clowns on election day or registering Darth Vader as a candidate may attract media attention.[4] Taking to public spaces to hold citizens' assemblies on election day would demonstrate the alternative. These ideas are only rudimentary – there is surely a multitude of ways to decry elections and build a movement that questions their efficacy.

One concern is that, by undermining elections, democracy itself will be undermined. Supporting democracy's foes, who often claim 'to be true friends of the people', must be avoided.[5] The campaign must make it clear that elections are to be replaced with sortition. The alternative conclusion to be drawn from demonstrating electoral democracy's failures, if sortition is not part of the message, is that democracy should be done away with altogether. Fortunately, democracy appears to 'thrive on imperfection'; the spur for improvement comes from a clear and popular understanding of the seriousness of its deficiencies.[6] And the direction of improvement is clear: sortition with deliberation.

The greater challenge is to make sortition the new norm. This is the flip side of delegitimising electoral politics – the feasible solution to the compelling problem. Promoting sortition as an alternative to elections will be a crucial aspect of change. The one place where random selection remains the accepted norm is in courtroom juries. Tying the legitimacy implied by the jury process to political legitimacy may be fruitful.

It was during the latter half of the 20th century that elections became the norm for selecting decision-makers for many groups of people. While elections have rarely infiltrated corporations or bureaucracies, where merit is supposedly the order of the day, elections became the default way various groups (clubs, societies, some not-for-profits) often choose their leaders. It may be difficult to supplant this ideal with that of random selection, especially among societies of volunteers where very differing levels of engagement, enthusiasm and commitment can occur.

However, it is already the case that many groups have a dedicated, elected secretariat (or executive) meeting regularly to decide operational matters, and a broader council amending or endorsing policy decisions, strategic directions and long-term plans. These councils could be replaced by a random selection of members, although the method of stratifying the random sample may be important here.[7] Internal biases in clubs and societies where the membership does not reflect the demographics of the constituency being served can easily occur. For example, the members of a charity for the homeless are rarely themselves homeless. If instituted, annual general meetings and the like could become far more than celebratory or reflective occasions, and turn into empowered decision-making conferences. Half the battle will be won when sortition is seen as the norm of legitimate decision-making across multiple spheres of public life. In Bolivia, the group Democracy In Practice is using sortition in student governance bodies; in Mexico, a poll found that over half (52 per cent) of those surveyed believed that citizens would govern better than politicians.[8] These are small but encouraging signs for the campaign for sortition.

Supporting and publicising alternatives that demonstrate the power of random selection is probably the best path towards normalising the practice. Every time a citizens' assembly occurs there is one more example to point to; every truly empowered policy jury will be one more demonstration that politicians are unnecessary; every successful deliberative poll gives more evidence that ordinary people, supported by good process, can deliberate effectively. Civil society groups such as the newDemocracy Foundation in Australia, the Jefferson Center in the US and the Dutch G1000 platform actively promote and organise these alternatives, providing a wealth of inspiration. Thomas Jefferson argued that democracy is something you can only learn by doing.[9]

Any event that encourages people to realise they can collectively make decisions without the need for elected leaders is another small step towards the goal. Replicating or extending the participatory budgeting processes already happening in many municipalities is an obvious place to begin. Start locally, in areas where people can directly experience the effects of participation. Then push for the many participatory budgeting processes to take control of a greater slice of the municipal budget. And if small-scale random selection is used in deciding service priorities, levels and funding sources across the full range of council services, which occurred in the municipality of Canada Bay in Sydney, Australia, in 2013, then this already represents a functioning model of a community parliament in miniature.[10]

Such assemblies should strive to be empowered: public meetings must be replaced by randomly selected people's advisory councils or juries – and then the word 'advisory' should be dropped. Developing a 'people's budget' to submit and compare with that of a relevant authority may be an interesting exercise, although people may be less willing to commit their time to something that does not have a guaranteed impact. Initially, many deliberative forums will be capacity-building, learning experiences. Keeping them local should mean they are more relevant and easier for the participants to engage with and understand the issues involved. Expanding their remit to cover a growing range of municipal activities, and introducing honorariums or per diem payments for participants, as in Fishkin's Deliberative Polling, and support for the inclusion of carers are almost the final steps: when one local council somewhere in the world is replaced (or accompanied) by a stratified random sample of people serving finite terms of office, then the first whiff of victory will be in the air.

What about confronting power? Is shattering the illusion of electoral democracy and mobilising support for the alternative enough? Can sortition be the Trojan Horse of a real democracy, wheeled into the state by politicians imagining it as a gift for solving so-called 'wicked problems' before they are ambushed and overthrown by its success?

As Bill McKibben, author and founder of the climate campaign group 350.org, points out:

> This fight, as it took me too long to figure out, was never going to be settled on the grounds of justice or reason. We won the argument, but that didn't matter: like most fights it was, and is, about power.[11]

If there are, as Erik Olin Wright argues, three main powers in society – economic, state and social – then perhaps 'desirable, viable, achievable' change will happen most easily only if there are alliances across these spheres.[12] More than likely, there is indeed 'strategic indeterminacy: there is no one way' to bring about change.[13]

With this caveat in mind, building a social movement to demand these changes – one that supports, mobilises, publicises and promotes real democracy – will surely help open up the political space for reform. This was already happening before the Occupy movement (and its predecessors, such as Los Indignados in Spain) flickered across the globe and exposed thousands, if not millions, to a critique of modern democracy and the ideals and problems of organising a people's assembly. By expanding these movements, or creating new ones, and bringing in a wide array of allies, the critique of electoral democracy could be pushed further to advocate the power of sortition.

Could a direct political arm of a movement for sortition, whose aims are to eliminate politicians and political parties, survive the contradictions and strains of participating in a system they are attempting to undermine and eliminate?

Interestingly, this is what happened in Kerala (a state of India with over 60 million people), Porto Alegre (Brazil) and Cotacachi (Ecuador).[14] In all these cases, established political parties of the left won elections on the promise to deliver power to the people. In Porto Alegre, it was the mayor from the Brazilian Workers' Party (Partido dos Trabalhadores) who initiated the first participatory budget process mentioned above. This process was located outside official state structures, meaning that final decision-making power continued to lie with the legislative assembly. However, the sheer weight of numbers of ordinary citizens involved, combined with the transparent process, bestowed a legitimacy on the resulting demands that the legislature could not defy.

From the history of modern democracy outlined in Part One, it is interesting to recall that often conservative politicians were the ones to expand the franchise. Politicians seek positions of power and, perhaps not so paradoxically, they may occasionally be willing to directly undermine their future prospects by offering concessions that they believe will deliver them to office today. 'With very rare exceptions, the right things are done for the wrong reasons,' wrote Saul Alinsky in 1971, and historical figures such as Benjamin Disraeli, a conservative politician who expanded the franchise significantly, are apt demonstrations of this occurring.[15] In an environment where most people despise politicians, a recurrent promise from many parties is to 'fix our politics', or 'do politics differently', or 'take back our government' – perhaps one day one of these politicians will be forced to fulfil this promise.[16]

In Europe and elsewhere, the Pirate Party has emerged as a manifestation of our networked society, and a reaction against restrictions on digital liberties. This technologically literate party is already experimenting with network forms of agenda- and policy-setting, some of them using interactive democracy software called Liquid Feedback, which is an online system for discussing, developing and either delegating or voting on proposals.

Although no Pirate Party has yet embraced sortition, political parties are beginning to appear that support the idea; before the Australian national election in 2013, The 23 Million party (23 million is the population of Australia) appeared with 'just one single goal: to secure a total review of the system of politics and government in Australia. And we want it carried out by a group of 150 randomly selected people from every corner of Australia, not by politicians.'[17] They did not last long, as the small group of volunteers was quickly overwhelmed by questions and supporters, and the demands of time, energy and money necessary for even the initial horse-trading in the allocation of preferences that is part of politics in the Australian Senate. In a real sense, they were a victim of their own (moderate) success. Several other very small political parties and independent candidates have explicitly run on a sortition platform, although none has yet come anywhere close to gaining office. The lesson to be learned here is that the better strategy may be to concentrate on convincing a well-established party to promote sortition, rather than starting a new party.

Even if there were only one well-resourced parliamentarian committed to sortition and deliberation who agreed to vote according to the outcome of a randomly selected deliberative assembly, then that single vote would represent the considered vote of the people. Such a politician may come from a party whose ultimate aim would be to amend electoral law (and constitutional law where necessary) to eliminate her or his position; it would be an anti-party full of un-politicians.

We should not, however, get carried away. Social and political movements are a necessary but not sufficient component of change. Real change comes with the widespread adoption of new behavioural norms. As Keane notes in relation to the US civil rights movement:

> It proved that the powerless had power to change things, and that change had to begin in the home, the workplace and in other public fields of everyday life, before spreading across the whole of the political and social landscape of the American democracy.[18]

Gutmann and Thompson see as desirable 'some substantial continuity between everyday life and political life... [with] a civil society that provides a rehearsal space for political deliberation'.[19] Or, as Carole Pateman puts it: 'Democratic ideals and politics have to be put into practice in the kitchen, the nursery and the bedroom.'[20] Real change is cultural change.

The seeds of this change, as we saw in Part Two, have already been planted. Collaborative networks supportive of diversity, using open standards and deliberation to produce immaterial goods – and laws are nothing if not immaterial – are already commonplace. In some schools, students deliberate together to determine a project-driven curriculum. The northern Italian city of Reggio Emilia is famous for this pedagogic innovation for preschool children (known as the Reggio Emilia Approach), and the techniques have been imitated worldwide and extended to higher-level students.

The network collaboration required to produce many products is building the capacity and expectations among many workers that participatory and empowered workplaces are possible. Within families, courses such as Parent Effectiveness Training (which began in the 1960s) strive to plough a middle path between authoritarian and permissive parenting – between total command and anything goes. Their principal technique is 'active listening', and the justifying and giving of mutually acceptable reasons and probable consequences – or deliberation by any other name.[21] In the book *Deliberative Systems* (edited by Parkinson and Mansbridge), deliberative democracy is said to be based on 'the intuition that being pressured into doing something and being persuaded into it are different. Deliberation is about genuine persuasion, not pressure.'[22] George Lakoff, in *The Political Mind*, outlines a direct analogy between mental models of idealised families and mental models of idealised national life, contrasting a Strict Father Model of appeals to authority and obedience with a Nurturing Parent Model appealing to explanation, care and restitution.[23] The parallels of the latter model with deliberative democracy are striking. If corporal punishment of children is taken as a primary example of strict authoritarian parenting, then every step away from it is hopefully a small step towards reasoned deliberation.

Not that anyone should expect a deliberative society to be an inevitable outcome of the emerging peer-to-peer network culture. The seed may have been planted, but it will need protection and nurturing to germinate. Deliberative democracy is more than a set of rules or procedures; it is a cultural disposition, and thus it is potentially a generational project. As stated above, it must bloom at home, at work and in our schools – a deliberative society will be created when we treat our children, our partners and our students, and bosses treat their employees, deliberatively.

Each time a parent, teacher, guardian or manager refuses to command, or refuses to reply to a 'Why?' with a 'Because I said so', and instead takes the time to offer intelligible justifications for decisions and listen to the responses – only then will the cultural change be well and truly under way. Only then will we be ready to legislate for ourselves.

Notes

1. Chris Rose, *How to Win Campaigns: Communications for Change*, second edition (Oneworld, 2010), 6.

2. The quote is from an extract from the book: http://www.theguardian.com/politics/2016/jun/29/why-elections-are-bad-for-democracy.

3. Van Reybrouck, *Against Elections*, 104.

4. Keane, Democracy, 759–61, lists several jokes and satirical election campaigns. Darth Vader campaign is here: https://www.washingtonpost.com/news/monkey-cage/wp/2015/10/30/yes-darth-vader-ran-for-office-in-ukraine-unfortunately-its-no-joke/.

5. Keane, *Democracy*, 813.

6. Keane, *Democracy*, 866.

7. Lyn Carson and Ron Lubensky, 'Appointments to Boards and Committees Via Lottery, a Pathway to Fairness and Diversity', *Journal of Public Affairs*, 2009, Vol. 9, 87–94.

8. Quoted in Keane, *Democracy*, 817.

9. Quoted in Hardt and Negri, *Commonwealth*, 310.

10. http://www.publicdeliberation.net/cgi/viewcontent.cgi?article=1238&context=jpd.

11. https://www.theguardian.com/environment/2015/mar/09/climate-fight-wont-wait-for-paris-vive-la-resistance.

12. Erik Olin Wright, *Envisioning Real Utopias* (Verso, 2010), 20.

13. Wright, *Envisioning*, 370.

14. T.M. Thomas Isaac and Patrick Heller, 'Democracy and Development: Decentralized Planning in Kerala', in Fung and Wright (eds), *Deepening Democracy*; and http://quod.lib.umich.edu/j/jii/4750978.0016.203/--participatory-democracy-in-ecuador?rgn=main;view=fulltext.

15. Saul Alinsky, *Rules for Radicals* (Random House, 1971), quoted in Rose, Campaigns, 6.

16. The first quote is from President Obama: http://www.nytimes.com/2016/01/14/us/politics/obama-state-of-the-union-republicans-democrats.html.

17. http://www.the23million.com.au/ (now closed down).

18. Keane, *Democracy*, 727.

19. Gutmann and Thompson, *Deliberative Democracy*, 35.

20. Carole Pateman, *The Disorder of Women: Democracy, Feminism, and Political Theory* (Stanford University Press, 1989), 222.

21. Thomas Gordon, *Parent Effectiveness Training: The Proven Program for Raising Responsible Children* (Harmony, 2000).

22. Parkinson and Mansbridge, *Deliberative Systems*, 18.

23. George Lakoff, *The Political Mind: A Cognitive Scientist's Guide to Your Brain and Its Politics* (Penguin, 2009).

Chapter 17: Ready for a Crisis

Crucial questions remain: is such change too radical a shift ever to occur? Although this project is grounded in the feasible, are we trying to climb a ladder to reach the stars? Are the forces that would unite in opposition to such a shift too powerful?

When, in Australia in 2010, Prime Minister Julia Gillard proposed a citizens' assembly on climate change, not only did the opposition rail against the idea, but virtually the entire chattering class of political journalists and commentators, shock jocks of conservative radio and television, and even the left-leaning Greens, attacked the proposal. An academic analysis of the media coverage of 'opinion leaders' divided the criticisms into procedural ('It will never work'), institutional ('It's a threat to democracy') and political objections (It's 'an abrogation of duty').[1] Although 'many of the arguments against the [citizens' assembly] are unfounded or misplaced', what is clear is that proposing the use of sortition is a highly political act that will encounter strong resistance across most, if not all, of the political spectrum.[2]

In Ireland, the year-long citizens' assembly that began in 2016 (and is ongoing as this book goes to press) is addressing several issues, including the constitutional ban on abortion. It has attracted vehement opposition from both the pro-life *and* pro-choice sides of the debate. The pro-life camp wants to maintain the status quo, the pro-choice side wants the ban addressed immediately, not at some uncertain time in the future after the conclusion of the assembly.[3] This uniting of previously antagonistic sides in opposition to the idea has strong parallels with what happened after the Australian assembly on climate change was proposed.

Handing power to the people is a political act; it threatens and challenges elite influence and the processes of elite bargaining. We must not presume it will be easy, and must be prepared to counter the opposition's arguments.

When you threaten someone's identity, someone's cherished dream come true (for politicians) and their status and access to power, you can only expect fierce reaction. If sortition does make inroads, then its foes will surely attempt to ridicule it, and try to corrupt and disrupt it wherever possible. When experts are shown to have fabricated results or to have presented a biased view, the media will jump on it as evidence of failure. The many times a randomly selected representative says something ridiculous, or is convicted of a criminal offence, or is shown to be fallibly human it will be splashed all over the front pages of the press, as it is now with politicians. Being prepared for setbacks such as these, and worse, and keeping on going, will be important. The level of animosity will be in direct proportion to the level of success; the surest sign that sortition is possible will be the virility of the attacks upon it – in a very real sense, heightened tension will be a cause for celebration.

The best answer to the question as to whether sortition is possible, and a deep source of motivation to continue promoting it, is the simple fact that it is already happening. These forums exist and they work, and every time they occur, society's collective capacity for deliberation is reinforced, the set of examples to point to is expanded and the conviction that sortition is a better way to do politics is justified. This is part of the well-worn path to social change: lobby governments, build a social movement, educate through doing and motivate people to normalise change. By now, the ball is on the move and picking up speed; we must keep kicking it along and keep pace with the movement.[4]

A significant crisis could, however, completely alter the political and socio-economic terrain.

Multiple crises occurring over a variety of uncertain timescales are breaking over us right now. Climate change is our species' 'catastrophe in slow motion'.[5] The rate at which we are exhausting the amount of easily attainable high-quality oil (the peak oil debate) is largely unknown, due in part to the political nature and secrecy of the major oil-producing nations. Hydraulic fracturing (or fracking) for non-conventional hydrocarbons, the exploitation of tar sands or more nuclear power plants may postpone the effects of peak oil, assuming the corporations responsible can continue to ignore or overcome widespread opposition, but the carbon-based activities will only accelerate the dangerous effects of spewing ever more pollutants into the atmosphere.

The structural issues that contributed to the financial crisis of 2007–8 and beyond, including too much debt, over-leveraged banks and irresponsible lending, remain largely unaddressed; it would seem global markets will be in for another bout of economic strife sooner or later.

The crises keep stacking up. Apocalypse is the new black: from movies to books to art, it is rapidly becoming banal to depict the end of the world.

Crisis also represents political opportunity. In Naomi Klein's 2008 book *The Shock Doctrine: The Rise of Disaster Capitalism*, several examples of the exploitation of crises to advance a (generally neoliberal) agenda are outlined.[6] Milton Friedman's famous quote from 1982 outlines the basic tactic:

> There is enormous inertia – a tyranny of the status quo – in private and especially governmental arrangements. Only a crisis – actual or perceived – produces real change. When that crisis occurs, the actions that are taken depend on the ideas that are lying around. That, I believe, is our basic function: to develop alternatives to existing policies, to keep them alive and available until the politically impossible becomes politically inevitable.[7]

Hardt and Negri agree:

> Even when tempted by despair, we should remember that throughout history unexpected and unforeseeable events arrive that completely reshuffle the decks of political powers and possibility. You don't have to be a millenarian to believe such events will come again… [so] our political task is paradoxical: we must prepare for the event even though its date of arrival remains unknown.[8]

This, then, is another possible tactic: keep the idea alive. Plan and hypothesise and strategise, and if the right moment comes, pounce. When the increase in extreme weather events, rising sea levels and other serious effects of climate change present themselves, and capitalism's most grave contradiction (the impossibility of continuous material growth on a finite planet) is laid bare, or the economic system undergoes major contraction or collapse, we must be ready: we must be ready to unfurl the sails so that when the wind of change blows we can harness its power and be carried to where we want to go. We must have examples to hand, have built a large and dedicated movement, and then push for the replacement of elections with sortition and the elimination of politicians – only then will we overcome the powerful lobbies and vested interests that would stop these crises being addressed.

Notes

1. John Boswell, Simon Niemeyer and Carolyn Hendriks, 'Julia Gillard's Citizens' Assembly Proposal for Australia: A Deliberative Democratic Analysis', *Australian Journal of Political Science*, Vol. 48, No. 2, 164–78.

2. John Boswell, Simon Niemeyer and Carolyn Hendriks, 'Julia Gillard's Citizens' Assembly Proposal for Australia: A Deliberative Democratic Analysis', *Australian Journal of Political Science*, Vol. 48, No. 2, 164–78.

3. https://www.opendemocracy.net/uk/brett-hennig/irish-citizens-assembly-on-abortion-democratisation-or-dodging-responsibility.

4. See, for example, Bill Moyer's *The Movement Action Plan* (second edition, 1986) for a model of popular social change – for example, from http://www.turning-the-tide.org/files/Moyers Movement Action Plan.pdf.

5. R. T. Pierrehumbert, 'Climate Change: A Catastrophe in Slow Motion', *Chicago Journal of International Law*, 2006, Vol. 6, No. 2.

6. Naomi Klein, *The Shock Doctrine: The Rise of Disaster Capitalism* (Penguin, 2008).

7. Milton Friedman, *Capitalism and Freedom: Fortieth Anniversary Edition* (University of Chicago Press, 2009), xiii–xiv.

8. Hardt and Negri, *Declaration*, 99–100.

Chapter 18: Justice? Or Just Us?

What about justice? Even if trust in politicians is at a historic low, and cynicism and indignation are common responses to most forms of politics, is the struggle for real democracy a progressive struggle? Will it advance justice, equality and freedom? Is it really desirable?

The populist critique of the elite control of government is also coming from the right of the political spectrum. Demands for less government interference, direct democracy through referenda and decentralisation can also be covers for austerity, fearmongering racism and the elimination of accountability and universally agreed standards and oversight.

Given that sortition is not strictly a project of the left or right, but the continuation of the democratic struggle for legitimacy, should we fear a dramatic swing to conservatism if it is implemented?

The evidence suggests otherwise. When the distribution of police resources in highly unequal regions of Chicago is put to a deliberative forum, it soon becomes impossible to justify neglecting areas of violent crime in favour of policing relatively safer wealthy neighbourhoods.[1] Participatory budgeting in Brazil draws participants as much from low-income areas as from their more wealthy counterparts. Unsurprisingly, the outcomes are generally redistributive: it is difficult to justify fixing your footpath if the people around the corner do not have access to clean water. Deliberative polls are regularly shown to produce progressive swings among the participants.

In *Declaration*, Michael Hardt and Antonio Negri agree that fixing our broken democracy is crucial for social justice: 'For all those who still hold passionately to the principles of freedom, equality, and the common, constituting a democratic society is the order of the day.'[2]

Archon Fung and Erik Olin Wright, the editors of *Deepening Democracy*, which presents and discusses numerous real-world examples of deliberation, put it this way:

> Since the idea of fairness is infused in the practice of reasonable discussion, truly deliberative decision-making should tend toward more equitable outcomes than those regulated by power, status, money, or numbers. There will

no doubt be some distance between this lofty deliberative
ideal and the actual practices of these experiments, but the
experiments should move decision-making closer to this
ideal than existing alternatives.[3]

There should be little doubt that if we wrestle the levers of government from the hands of the (generally) old, white and rich men, and
place them in the hands of an informed representative sample of the
entire adult population, things will get less comfortable for the very
rich and much fairer for the other 99 per cent. When almost the entire
parliament is composed of workers and carers, with a sprinkling of
financial traders and managers, what kind of legislation is likely to
be passed? A recent US study and related video highlighted significant differences between the *actual* distribution of wealth in the US
(extremely unequal) and what people *think* it is (they think it is very
unequal), and between what they *think* it is and what they consider
an *ideal* distribution to be (somewhat unequal). When presented with
unlabelled wealth distribution pie charts and asked to choose where
they would prefer to live, 47 per cent preferred Sweden's distribution,
43 per cent an equal (socialist) distribution and only 10 per cent said
they would prefer to live in a country with the US's highly unequal
wealth distribution.[4] This is where informed deliberation comes in.
If misconceptions were corrected and people were asked to deliberate about what kind of society they wanted to live in, it appears there
would be a remarkable degree of agreement about the desire to live
with a far more equitable distribution of wealth than currently exists.

Richard Wilkinson and Kate Pickett, in *The Spirit Level: Why
Greater Equality Makes Societies Stronger*, present a plethora of data
showing how income inequality is strongly correlated to a host of
health and social problems. They conclude: 'Greater equality is the
gateway to a society capable of improving the quality of life for all of
us and an essential step in the development of a sustainable economic
system.'[5] They argue that the single most effective way of improving
social and health outcomes is by reducing inequality, which, according to the study above, is also a very popular, widespread desire. Furthermore, Wilkinson and Pickett state that: 'The evidence strongly
suggests that narrowing income differences within rich countries will
make them more responsive to the needs of poorer countries.'[6] More
equal countries tend to redistribute more to poorer countries, so
reducing national inequality should lead to reduced global inequality
as well.

Sortition, by making government responsive to the informed wishes of a representative sample of people, should produce a more equal society, and thus a happier, healthier society and world.

Not that consensus about a problem, such as inequality, equates to consensus on its causes, or potential solutions. However, it is not hard to imagine who might be taxed more, and who less, if a representative sample of people had the power to decide these matters for themselves.

In many controversial areas, informed deliberation should produce progressive outcomes, if only because the Index of Ignorance (a creation of the market research organisation Ipsos MORI), which measures the gap between perception and reality, is often very high. When people in the UK were asked what percentage of the UK population are immigrants, the mean response from unprompted answers was 31 per cent, whereas the actual figure is 13 per cent. They further estimated that 21 per cent of the immigrants were asylum seekers; the actual figure is four per cent.[7] Other areas with a high ignorance index are the number of teenage births and the percentage of Muslims in Western societies.[8] The correction of these gross misunderstandings, and the reliance on facts (rather than opinions), would surely have a positive effect on the policies made by a group of deliberating, randomly selected citizens.

Do we have faith in ordinary people? When put in positions of responsibility, given access to our best efforts at providing unbiased information and engaged in a balanced process of reasoned, moral deliberation, they would surely decide to stop pumping so much pollution into our atmosphere and critically changing the chemical composition of the air we need to survive. In deliberative forums in the US, people demand less military expenditure. A parliament of workers and carers would most likely protect workers' rights, provide payments to carers and tax the wealthy. They could instigate not only a universal basic income and minimum living wage, but also a maximum wage, denying that CEOs deserve to be paid hundreds of times the pay of an average worker. Imagine a global, randomly selected people's assembly where everyday, hard-working and sympathetic participants from the developed world could deliberate face to face with the impoverished and undernourished of our planet. Will the well-off be able to justify to themselves and, more importantly, to everybody else in such a public forum, that limiting the global redistribution of wealth to its current pitiful levels, and underfunding access to health, clean water and education for much of humanity, is a necessary evil if our own national economies are to continue thriving and our standard of living is to be maintained?

The increased legitimacy of sortition will lead to more justice and more equality. It is time for ordinary people to deliberate together, with experts informing them and independent facilitators helping them to arrive at the moral crux of decisions, and from there to decide what the best policies are to guide us collectively. Let us harness the ideals of the information revolution and use the power of networks to realise the remarkable promise of democracy whispered in the ear of society throughout the ages: that we can decide what the good life is, together, as equals.

Notes

1. Fung and Wright (eds), *Deepening Democracy*, Chapter Four.

2. Hardt and Negri, *Declaration*, 100.

3. Fung and Wright (eds), *Deepening Democracy*, 26.

4. Michael I. Norton and Dan Ariely, 'Building a Better America – One Wealth Quintile at a Time', *Perspectives on Psychological Science*, 2011, Vol. 6, 9; also see the related YouTube video: http://www.youtube.com/watch?v=QPKKQnijnsM that had over 16 million views by January 2015.

5. Richard Wilkinson and Kate Pickett, *The Spirit Level: Why Greater Equality Makes Societies Stronger* (Bloomsbury Press, 2010), 232.

6. Wilkinson and Pickett, *The Spirit Level*, 229.

7. http://www.ipsos-mori.com/Assets/Docs/Polls/ipsos-mori-rss-kings-perils-of-perception-topline.pdf. However, there are some strange figures in these results: 24 per cent declined to guess how many immigrants there are in the UK, while the second-largest category (12 per cent) guessed that more than 51 per cent of the population were not born in the UK.

8. https://www.ipsos-mori.com/researchpublications/researcharchive/3466/Perceptions-are-not-reality-10-things-the-world-gets-wrong.aspx.

Thanks for reading *The End of Politicians: Time for a Real Democracy*.
If you want to see the ideas in this book
become more than words, please join the
Sortition Foundation
www.sortitionfoundation.org
facebook.com/SortitionFoundation
twitter.com/SortitionNow

Acknowledgements

Many people helped this book become what it is today. Numerous conversations, heated discussions, campfire rants and quiet words with attendees at various workshops and conferences helped me massage the ideas into the form in which they now appear. The book started off as a very different beast, and took some years to tame. Very early drafts of the book were put through several long, after-dinner conversations with Laurel, Bec, Raf, Theo and Roger – thanks for persisting! Later drafts were read by Lyn Carson, Manuel Arriaga, Eric Olin Wright, Bettina Wittneben, John Gastil and Yoram Gat. Their enthusiasm was almost as invaluable as their comments. I must also thank those practitioners of sortition-based experiments who responded to my queries, gave me advice and allowed me to comprehend the immense effort required to use sortition successfully: Cato Léonard from the Belgian G1000, Iain Walker and Lyn Carson from the newDemocracy Foundation, and Harm van Dijk and Jerphaas Donner from the Dutch G1000 platform. Even so, the manuscript might have languished on my laptop if not for the infectious excitement of a bunch of Lugaro: Silvio, Mariateresa and Carlo. You gave me faith when my own was waning. Further thanks go to my editors, Richard Collins, who helped me step back and see the work with more critical eyes, and Ian Critchley, for improving the manuscript in a hundred small but important ways. And, finally, thanks to Unbound and all those supporters who pledged and made the crowdfunding campaign on Unbound a success – without you the book would never have been published.

Select Bibliography

This is not a comprehensive biography, but a short list of references that I consider the most important and interesting. For the full list, see the notes.

Achen, Christopher H. and Bartels, Larry M. *Democracy for Realists: Why Elections Do Not Produce Responsive Government* (Princeton University Press, 2016).

Amadae, S.M. *Rationalizing Capitalist Democracy: The Cold War Origins of Rational Choice Liberalism* (University of Chicago Press, 2003).

Bartels, Larry M. *Unequal Democracy: The Political Economy of the New Gilded Age* (Princeton University Press, 2010).

Castells, Manuel. *The Information Age: Economy, Society and Culture. Volume 1: The Rise of the Network Society*, second edition (Blackwell, 2000).

Colomer, Josep M. *Political Institutions: Democracy and Social Choice* (Oxford University Press, 2001).

Dahl, Robert A. *On Democracy* (Yale University Press, 1998).

Dryzek, John S. with Niemeyer, Simon. *Foundations and Frontiers of Deliberative Governance* (Oxford University Press, 2010).

Dunn, John. *Democracy: A History* (Atlantic Monthly Press, 2005).

Fishkin, James. *When the People Speak: Deliberative Democracy and Public Consultation* (Oxford University Press, 2011).

Fung, Archon and Wright, Erik Olin (eds). *Deepening Democracy: Institutional Innovations in Empowered Participatory Governance* (Verso, 2002).

Gastil, John and Levine, Peter (eds). *The Deliberative Democracy Handbook: Strategies for Effective Civic Engagement in the 21st Century* (Jossey-Bass, 2005).

Gilens, Martin. *Affluence and Influence: Economic Inequality and Political Power in America* (Princeton University Press, 2014).

Gutmann, Amy and Thompson, Dennis. *Why Deliberative Democracy?* (Princeton University Press, 2004).

Hardt, Michael and Negri, Antonio. *Commonwealth* (Harvard University Press, 2009).

Hardt, Michael and Negri, Antonio. *Empire* (Harvard University Press, 2000).

Hardt, Michael and Negri, Antonio. *Multitude: War and Democracy in the Age of Empire* (Penguin, 2005).

Hobsbawm, Eric. *The Age of Capital: 1848–1875* (Abacus, 1997).

Hobsbawm, Eric. *The Age of Empire: 1875–1914* (Abacus, 1994).

Hobsbawm, Eric. *The Age of Extremes: The Short Twentieth Century, 1914–1991* (Abacus, 1995).

Hobsbawm, Eric. *The Age of Revolution: 1789–1848* (Abacus, 1977).

Hugo, Victor. *Les Misérables* (Penguin, 1982).

Keane, John. *The Life and Death of Democracy* (W. W. Norton, 2009).

King, Anthony. *Who Governs Britain?* (Pelican, 2015).

Landemore, Hélène. *Democratic Reason: Politics, Collective Intelligence, and the Rule of the Many* (Princeton University Press, 2012).

Manin, Bernard. *The Principles of Representative Government* (Cambridge University Press, 1997).

OECD Studies on Public Engagement. *Focus on Citizens: Public Engagement for Better Policy and Services* (OECD, 2009).

Orwell, George. 'Politics vs. Literature: An Examination of Gulliver's Travels', *Polemic* (1946: 5).

Page, Scott E. *The Difference: How the Power of Diversity Creates Better Groups, Firms, Schools and Societies* (Princeton University Press, 2007).

Phillips, Anne. *The Politics of Presence* (Oxford University Press, 1995).

Rose, Chris. *How to Win Campaigns: Communications for Change*, second edition, (Oneworld, 2010).

Shapiro, Ian; Stokes, Susan C.; Wood, Elizabeth J.; and Kirchner, Alexander S. (eds). *Political Representation* (Cambridge University Press, 2009).

Shirky, Clay. *Here Comes Everybody: The Power of Organizing Without Organizations* (Allen Lane, 2008).

Smith, Graham. *Democratic Innovations* (Cambridge University Press, 2009).

Van Reybrouck, David. *Against Elections: The Case for Democracy* (Bodley Head, 2016).

Wilkinson, Richard and Pickett, Kate. *The Spirit Level: Why Greater Equality Makes Societies Stronger* (Bloomsbury Press, 2010).

Patrons List

Carlo Abate
George Angelou
Marc Artzrouni
Nesher Asner
Anthony Barnett
The Bazeley Family
Neal Beets
Nanni Bianchi
Valentina Bianco
Brigid & Bingo Blakeney
Roger Blunden
Gail Bradbrook
Jane Brant
Luke Buckland
Marcus Butcher
Aifric Campbell
Daniel Campbell-Macdonald
Anthony Carrick
Joanna Cary
Willie Catchpool
Patrick Chalmers
Helen Christensen
Alan Constantine
Marco Cossu
Cory Cox
Péter Dóczi
Carolyn Doherty
Madeleine Egan
Tristan Epstein
Oliver Escobar
Paul Evans
Teigan Evans
Bianca Festa
Sadie Few
Richard Fox
Sue Fry
Andrew Goltz

Michael Green
James Harvey
Christine Hastie
Zoe Hayman
Peter Hennig
Rachel Hennig
Colin Hill
Melinda Jenei-Majlath
Andrea Jouve
Daniel Kelliher
Amrit Khalsa
Richard Knights
Martin Knox
Soeren Larsen
Zii Liguriani
Megan Lloyd
Jamie Logan
Giovanni Lugaro
Dennis Luts
Rosemary Mardling
Jim Mooney
Bec Nissen
Liam O'Mahoney
Therese O'Mahoney
Kalman 'Sergeant' Perenyi
Nick Pruet
Nik Rawlinson
Tyrone Reitman
Veruska & Riccardo
Rich Rippin
Gary Robbins
Gallino Roberto
Malcolm Saunders
Julia Schindler
Guilherme Serodio
Liz Shield
Paul Simpson
Marion Singer
Graham Smith
Christopher Tout
Luca Valerio

Greg Wierzbicki
John Wills